Famous People You Might Meet in Eternity

TONY A. POWERS

ISBN 978-1-0980-7321-3 (paperback)
ISBN 978-1-0980-7322-0 (digital)

Christian Faith Publishing, Inc.
832 Park Avenue
Meadville, PA 16335
www.christianfaithpublishing.com

Printed in the United States of America

To my beloved wife, Connie, who does everything for me.

eternity (n). Infinite duration, without beginning in the past or end in the future; endless time.

—*Webster's Dictionary*

CONTENTS

PROLOGUE

Former sportscaster Tony Powers lay down on the chilly cross-shaped operating table for what he thought would be routine minor meniscus knee surgery. He thought how strange it was for the operating table to be shaped like a giant cross. He thought of Jesus being crucified. A young surgical nurse appeared dressed in all-green hospital digs. She held a large rubber mask, which she placed over Tony's face, and asked him to breathe deep. He took a few nervous breaths, and after a couple of minutes, everything seemed to turn into a black void.

He felt like an astronaut being whisked into outer space from Cape Kennedy. He could see Mother Earth, and it looked like the beautiful blue globe he'd seen on television many times. It seemed to vibrate, and he could see the oceans and continents below. He gazed upward into outer space and the heavens. He couldn't believe his eyes. There were people all lined up, millions of them.

He watched wave after wave of them walking in lines toward a brilliantly illuminated cloud in the distance. There they disappeared after entering the cloud. Some of the people he recognized were famous coaches, presidents, professional athletes, actors, actresses, politicans, generals, and historical figures. Like a true sportscaster, he had interviewed a few of them. There were peoples of all colors, creeds, and ages. Some spoke to him and some didn't. Everyone he conversed with had the same answer. They wished they could have lived their lives on earth all over again.

Tony met former president Ronald Reagan in eternity. They both had worked for the same radio station, WHO Radio in Des

Moines. When their visit ended, President Reagan handed Tony three jelly beans as a keepsake. Their colors were red, white, and blue. Tony vowed he'd cherish them forever.

Was all this just an anesthesia-induced dream or a figment of his imagination? Had he been carried into the heavens suspended between life and death? Had Tony been thrust into the third dimension known as the Twilight Zone?

Had Tony Powers crossed into eternity?

The answer will surprise you.

CHAPTER 1

Famous People You Might
Meet in Eternity

I think I might have died.

Don't go feeling sorry for me. It wasn't that bad. I went in for arthroscopic knee surgery, and they put me under. I just didn't wake up. That's all. It happens to the best of us. When your time is up, it's up. The last person I saw alive was a pretty nurse who placed an oxygen mask over my face and told me to breathe deep. Then it was like a dream.

It was beautiful. The heavens, I mean. Death is really an out-of-this-world experience. You're like an astronaut suspended in deep space and you can see our magnificent earth far below you. Thousands, make that millions, of people were all in these huge processions that moved slowly toward a distant, blindingly bright light in the middle of a huge white cloud. It reminded me of the Steven Spielberg movie *Close Encounters of the Third Kind.* The light was so brilliant that you had to shield your eyes to see, like actor Richard Dreyfus encountering the alien visitors.

People of all nationalities and colors proceeded slowly as far you could see. Some were Africans dressed in their best tribal clothes. Americans, Britishers, Russians, Saudis, Israelis, Africans, African Americans, Hispanics, Caucasians, Chinese, Muslims, Japanese, and Indians were there in all age groups. Many wore their Sunday finest clothes of suits and dresses while others looked like they didn't have time to dress up. Small children with wings like little guardian angels patiently urged folks to keep moving. In the distance there was a magnificent rainbow with a plethora of colors; it took your breath away, no pun intended.

There were loud blasts from trumpets, pipe organ music, and lots of singing. But it wasn't obtrusive. It was like hearing the Mormon Tabernacle Choir in concert. There was no explanation needed. We were all headed to judgment day. I figured it would take me years just to get to the front of the line. No one seemed to be in any big hurry. In eternity, you have all the time in the world, again no pun intended.

It wasn't long before I started to recognize faces of some of the people walking beside me. Some cajoled and laughed like they were out taking an evening stroll while others stared silently and blankly ahead. It was as if they knew what their judgment would be. I noticed the Duke, John Wayne, dressed in a fancy Western-style shirt adorned with lassos and black shiny cowboy boots. The Duke passed in 1979. I remember seeing him live while visiting WMAQ-TV in Chicago in 1978. He was a huge man with large hands. I had said hi to him as he walked into the station, and he had winked and waved at me and my wife, Connie.

In eternity, he wore a brown cowboy hat and had a gold belt buckle in the shape of a horse. I thought his finest movie performance was *The Searchers*. He walked side by side with Jimmy Stewart, who died in 1997. Jimmy wore a red-and-black checkered shirt and wore brown cowboy boots with spurs. He was great as Charles Lindbergh in *The Spirit of St. Louis*. I eavesdropped a little on their conversation.

"Eastwood made too many of those spaghetti Westerns, Jimmy," the Duke said. "We made real Western movies."

"Yup, yup," Stewart replied. "We'll have to kid him about it when he finally arrives up here."

I was in absolute awe when Albert Einstein walked by engrossed with a laptop computer and dressed in a brilliant all-white suit. He had passed on in 1955. Should I interview him? I wondered. I decided not to because I really didn't know what to ask such a brilliant man.

I was shocked to see the premier of the former Soviet Union, Nikita Krushchev, wander by. He had passed away in 1971. I was just a youngster when he told some of the world's leaders during the Cold War, "We Will Bury You," in the late 1950s.

I saw a gentleman walk by wearing a blue flight suit with a dark blue NASA patch on front. Inscribed on the patch were the words "Apollo 13" with a bright white rocket encircling the globe. His name tag identified him as astronaut John "Jack" Swigert, one of the Apollo 13 crew in 1970. He had died in 1982. I'll never forget those famous words, "Houston, we have a problem," when one of the oxygen tanks exploded on the Apollo 13 mission. Swigert, along with fellow astronauts Jim Lovell and Fred Haise, had to construct an emergency oxygen system to make it back to earth alive and cancel their trip to the moon.

Many recognizable faces streamed by. There was Clark Gable, who died in 1960; Dale Earnhardt, who was killed tragically in 2001; Johnny Carson, who passed in 2005; the great Martin Luther King Jr., who was assassinated in 1968; and his beautiful wife, Coretta Scott King, who passed away in 2006. They all walked by me and nodded hello. I said hi to all of them. I noticed Joan Rivers, who passed on in 2014, just before my knee surgery. She cracked jokes even in death.

She looked me over up and down then smiled. She noticed my skimpy hospital garb, which consisted of a green hospital gown, a green mesh to cover my hair, and a flimsy pair of slippers.

"Who's your tailor, sir? I'd fire him," she said. "You do have underwear on, don't you? Jesus better not see you dressed in that outfit," she said with a chuckle. She then moved on and disappeared.

I froze and was startled when I recognized President John Fitzgerald Kennedy, the thirty-fifth president of the United States. He was the youngest president to be elected at age forty-three and the youngest to die in office in 1963. He looked very presidential and wore a black leather jacket that said "Commander in Chief" on the front. It bore the seal of the President of the United States. I said hi to him. He smiled and said hi back to me.

"I voted for you," I said not knowing what else to say.

"Thank you," he replied with a smile. "You must have been around thirteen years old when you voted," he said with that famous Kennedy grin and accent.

I was amazed that he figured out how old I was when he was elected in 1960. Did he possess some uncanny mental telepathy or something? I thought.

"What's your name?" he asked.

"Tony Powers, Mr. President. I was a radio and television sportscaster when I was alive."

"Really, that's a nice occupation and name," he said. "You could have run for political office with a name like that. Let me guess, you must have died while in the hospital."

"I went in for minor knee surgery, Mr. President, and never woke up."

"I'm real sorry, Tony. My chronic bad back nearly killed me in the White House," he said with a wink and a smile.

"I'm sorry you were assassinated," I blurted out.

He stared at me for a moment like I had just made a real dumb reporter's statement or something like that. His eyes turned moist.

"It really doesn't matter much now, does it," he said.

I could see he was a little disappointed that I had mentioned how he died. I could have kicked myself for doing so. I was a high school student at the time and didn't really realize the gravity of what had happened in Dallas. I had always felt the Russians were responsible for his death. He made them look bad after he had told them to get their missiles out of Cuba.

"Hey, it was great to meet you, Tony," he said finally. "I suppose I'd better move on and find Jackie, John Jr., Bobby, and Ted. I hope to see you again at the top."

"Goodbye, Mr. President," I said.

He walked off ahead of me and soon disappeared into the crowd. I was mad at myself for my classless observation that had brought an end to our conversation. I vowed that if I saw him again in eternity, I would apologize to him. Why didn't I just tell him that he was one of the greatest presidents ever? I always remembered his classic speech: "Ask not what your country can do for you, ask what you can do for your country."

I reconnoitered for more familiar faces and saw Pope John Paul II dressed in magnificent papal attire. He had passed away in 2005. What a great person, I thought. He was canonized a saint in the Roman Catholic Church. Why would God even need to judge him? I wondered. Napoleon Bonaparte rode by on a great big white stallion. He had passed on in 1821. Julius Caesar, killed in 44 BC strode by dressed in a brown leather Roman soldier's uniform with gold chest and shoulder protectors. He was followed by General George Armstrong Custer attired in his U.S. Seventh Cavalry's blues. He was killed by the Sioux in 1876. Custer had blond, shoulder-length hair, and a monstrous mustache. I often wondered how such a military genius could have been outsmarted by the Sioux in the massacre at Little Bighorn.

I did a double take at the next individual I saw. A nice-looking young man ambled up. He wore an old WWII aviator's helmet with a white scarf and a black sweater with a gold letter "I" sewn on the front. He carried a football. I recognized him immediately from photos I had seen.

Three yards from me stood one of the greatest athletes in Iowa history. I couldn't believe it.

It was Nile Kinnick.

CHAPTER 2

Nile Kinnick

"You're Nile Kinnick," I said. "They named the University of Iowa stadium after you in 1972, and there's a street named in your honor in your hometown of Adel, Iowa. It's called Nile Kinnick Drive. I drove on it a few times. I'm from Iowa too."

His face lit up with recognition when I mentioned Iowa.

"Were you an Iowa Hawkeye fan?" he asked.

"Well, kind of. I'm Tony Powers and I worked as a sportscaster with Jim Zabel at WHO Radio and TV in Des Moines. Jim and one of your teammates named Al Couppee talked about you often. Al gave me my start in broadcasting at KGTV in San Diego where he was the sports director. He constantly talked about you and said if you had lived, you would have become a future president of the United States. I worked for him about two years.

"Jim hired me and I moved back to Iowa and covered Iowa football at Kinnick Stadium in the late 1970s and all of the '80s. Hayden Fry was the head coach then. They made a big bronze bust of you that sits outside the stadium. You're a real legend in Iowa, Mr. Kinnick, and I've read several books about your life."

"Call me Nile," he said. "So you worked with Al. He was the quarterback on our 1939 Ironmen team. He was a real rough tough guy and a Navy veteran. What's he doing now?"

I looked around at the mass of humanity that moved by us.

"I think he's up here somewhere with us. Al passed away in 1998, and Jim died in 2013, last year. Maybe we should look around and try to find them up here," I replied.

"We've got plenty of time for that," he said. "My life ended pretty abruptly and, as you can see, I'm still making my way to judgment."

He held out a weathered football that looked like one used in the 1930s.

"You want to play some catch?"

"Won't we lose our place in line?" I asked.

He chuckled.

"As I said, we've got plenty of time for that. You forget we're in eternity."

We found a meadow that I swear resembled the Garden of Eden. Luscious-looking fruit hung from the apple and pear trees. I didn't know you could be hungry when you were dead. I noticed a few huge snakes curled around some of the tree branches. There was a rectangular field with the greenest grass you could ever imagine, all nicely cut and trimmed like a football gridiron. All that was missing were the goalposts and bleachers. Around the field was a scattered cornucopia of beautiful impatiens, wildflowers, daylilies, and wild roses. There were nearby fields of glorious yellow sunflowers all opened up and pointed toward the heavens like souls ready to be called up. You couldn't think of a better place to play catch with the great Nile Kinnick.

I have to admit it was a little rough to run some short pass patterns in my hospital garb and injured knee, but Kinnick threw nice soft passes with a tight spiral. He even ran a few pass patterns himself and was so fast that I underthrew him. He wasn't a very big guy, maybe one hundred seventy pounds, but he made up for it with speed and quickness. I tried to work up the nerve to ask him about his death. I didn't want to make the same mistake that I made with President Kennedy. Finally I thought I'd be very diplomatic.

"Nile, do you mind if I ask you a personal question?" I asked.

He started to throw another short pass but paused and reflected a moment like he'd read my mind.

"I know. You want to know how I died," he said. "I'll tell you. It happened June 2, 1943. I was almost twenty-five and a Naval aviator on the USS *Lexington*. I took off on a training flight over the Gulf of Paria in Venezuela. My plane started to leak tons of oil. I had no choice but to ditch. The problem is if you don't land on water just right, it's like crashing into concrete. The impact probably knocked me out and I drowned when the plane went under. I see they never recovered my body. Can I ask what happened to you?"

"I went in for a minor knee repair and the anesthesia killed me."

"My God, you've got to be kidding me," he laughed.

His laugh was contagious. He pointed at my hospital gown.

"They could have at least provided you with some decent traveling clothes," he mused.

"I'd give anything for a decent shirt and a pair of pants," I deadpanned.

We continued to play some catch, and I asked him about his 1939 Heisman Trophy.

"Your Heisman Trophy speech was pretty special and very good. It was very patriotic. I've heard it several times."

He stopped throwing and stared at me for a moment with sad eyes. I could see that it was hard for him to talk about the award and his life, which ended tragically when he was so young.

"I wanted to live and become a lawyer and possibly a politician. I wanted to marry and have a great life on earth, but that didn't happen. Don't get me wrong. I was glad to have won the Heisman and died while serving my country, but life's so precious." His voice trailed off. "I wish God had let me live, but that wasn't in his great plan. If I could have flown back to the carrier, I think I could have landed the plane. Oh well, I could have been killed later in a dogfight or something like that. What year did you die?"

"This year, 2014."

I watched him as he figured in his head.

"My God, I've been dead seventy-one years," he replied. "It's like it happened yesterday, and I still haven't made it to judgment day. I've been on that road seventy-one years and still have a long ways to go. It's like time stood still up here. I wonder when I'll finally get there. Heck, I'm in no hurry. Tell me, what were the Iowa campus and stadium like when you last saw it?"

"It's a beautiful campus, you'd think you were in heaven," I said with a chuckle. "The old capitol is still there with a gold dome, and they remodeled Iowa—I mean Kinnick Stadium. It seats seventy thousand now, and there is a magnificent press box with suites. The University of Iowa Hospital sits right across the street from the stadium and is one of the best hospitals in the nation.

"There are now fourteen teams in the Big Ten Conference with two divisions. Iowa and Minnesota are in the west division. Nebraska, Maryland, and Rutgers all joined the conference. The Big Ten now stretches across two thirds of the country. There are what they call the Power Five conferences now in college football—the Big Ten, Big-12, Pac-12, Southeastern Conference, and Atlantic Coast Conference. At the end of the season, the top four teams will play for the national title. They even have instant replay. The games are recorded, and officials can review controversial calls."

He lofted another short pass toward me.

"Wow, really," he said. "What about Notre Dame?"

"They're still an independent in football and they have their own television network just like the Big Ten. Iowa and Notre Dame quit playing each other in the early 1960s. What was your favorite game in that 1939 season?"

My question seemed to elate him; he beamed happily.

"Oh, when we beat Notre Dame seven to six. That was probably my best game. It was such a great rivalry. There were many great memories that season, and all the Ironmen were pretty special. I hope I bump into Al and my other teammates soon up here."

We continued to throw a few more passes, and he talked lovingly about growing up in his hometown of Adel and his student days at Iowa. It was such a shame that his life was cut so short. You could see that, had he lived, he would have done something else remarkable in his life, such as become President of the United States or a powerful U.S. senator. The Heisman Trophy would have been gravy.

I told him how much I admired him and how I grew up on an Iowa farm and listened to Jim Zabel announce Hawkeye football on WHO Radio. There wasn't a broadcast when the name Nile Kinnick wasn't mentioned in some way.

"I wish I could have done play-by-play while you were at Iowa," I said. "I would have announced: *Kinnick drops straight back to pass against the Irish, there's a heavy rush by Notre Dame, he escapes and starts to run. He's at the forty...the fifty...the forty...he stiff-arms a tackler at the thirty and he breaks into the clear...he's going to score... Touchdown Iowa!*"

"Hey, you're a good announcer," he said with a hearty laugh.

"And you're the only Heisman Trophy winner to have a stadium named after you," I added.

"Oh, wow," he answered. "If only I had lived. Life would have been so different."

He smiled again but then suddenly ended our throwing session. He walked up to me and thrust out his right hand.

"Tony, it was great to meet you and throw the pigskin around. I wish I had known you on earth. I'm sorry your life had to end."

"If you ever see Al or Jim Zabel," I replied, "tell each of them thank you for helping me get into sports broadcasting. I'm eternally grateful."

"I certainly will, and thank you, Tony, for telling me they named Iowa Stadium after me and a street in my hometown of Adel. And about all those super conferences and instant replay. Wow, that made my day, I mean my eternity," he said with a big smile.

"Goodbye," he said. He walked off the field and soon merged back into the crowd. He'd toss the football into the air and catch it again and again.

I thought I heard him whistle as he walked away. It must have made him very happy to talk about Iowa football. He'd travel into eternity with the knowledge that he was immortalized forever.

I stood there and watched him until he disappeared, then trudged back into line myself.

I felt sad for a moment but then happy. I had just become friends with one of the greatest Iowans ever.

CHAPTER 3

Here's Johnny—Johnny Orr

I just about died (wait a minute; I'm already dead, aren't I?) when I saw former Michigan and Iowa State basketball coach Johnny Orr as he stood in line. We made eye contact at about the same time. He wore an expensive gray suit with a cardinal-and-gold tie. He looked like a million bucks and appeared at least ten to fifteen years younger than his eighty-six years of age. He recognized me and came over. He grasped my right hand and shook it heartily.

"Hey, coach, what are you doing up here?" he asked. He'd addressed everybody as "coach" when he was alive.

"I died about a year after you, coach, this year in 2014."

"You're way too young to be dead," he said as he eyed my green hospital shirt.

"I'm sorry you passed away, coach. You were an iconic legend at Iowa State and Michigan."

"Well, I tripped and fell and hit my head and that was it," he said. "Besides, they turned the basketball program over to a guy who could outcoach me in a minute, coach, one of my former players Fred Hoiberg. Man, can he coach. He played in the NBA, man, just like Jeff Hornacek and Jeff Grayer. They were great too. Say, what happened to you?" he asked in his graveled voice.

"I went in for knee surgery. They put me under and I never woke up."

He stared at me with a look of pity in his eyes.

"Sorry to hear that, coach," he said.

"You wouldn't believe who I just talked to, Johnny."

"Who's that, coach?"

"Nile Kinnick."

"You're kidding me, coach. You saw the great Nile Kinnick? Wow, I'd love to meet him."

I still couldn't quite believe I was having a conversation with the great Johnny Orr. He was a coaching legend in the 1970s at Michigan before Iowa State stole him away from the Wolverines. I attended the news conference in 1980 when ISU announced Johnny as its new coach.

"Coach, I remember when I attended your press conference in 1980 when Iowa State hired you as coach. You surprised the basketball world and media when you left Michigan," I said.

"Coach, I was as surprised as you were when Iowa State offered me the job. Lou McCollough was the athletic director. He called me and asked if I knew anybody who would be interested in the Iowa State job. He was kind of interested in my assistant coach, Bill Frieder. Heck, I asked Lou what the ISU job paid. He told me. I was immediately interested and said I'd like to throw my hat into the ring. I made peanuts at Michigan, and when Iowa State hired me, they made me a millionaire."

Johnny went on to become the winningest coach in ISU history with 218 victories. We reminisced about his greatest victories at Iowa State.

"Oh, when we beat Michigan in the 1986 NCAA tournament," Orr said. "That was probably my biggest win. When we beat Danny Manning and Kansas, that was pretty sweet too. They were all good. But I had a great life, coach. All the money and fame don't do you a bit of good up here, coach. I tried to make all of my players good citizens and people. I hope the Good Lord gave me credit for that."

"He will, Johnny, I'm sure of it. Coach, you sure gave the fans goosebumps when you came out before games at Hilton Coliseum with those pumped fists and the band played the 'Here's Johnny' theme song from the *Tonight Show*. That really fired up the crowd," I said.

"That was fun, coach, wasn't it?" he said. "I mean, there was something to that Hilton magic they always talked about. The roar of the crowd was like having a sixth man on the floor. It won a lot of games for us there. Oh man, if only I could go back," he said with a forlorn look on his face.

We had a great visit about ISU basketball, and then our conversation switched from basketball to golf. He was as good a golfer as he was basketball coach.

"Johnny, do you think they have a golf course up here somewhere for us? I remember the old Death Valley Open golf days at the Veenker Golf Course in Ames in hot August. The local media would team up with the ISU coaches for an eighteen-hole best ball match. Everybody wanted to be in your foursome, coach. You were a scratch golfer, and your teams always won the tournament and the top prizes."

He gazed up at the long lines of people ahead of us that stretched far up into the heavens.

"It's going to be a while before we get up there, coach," he said, "so we might as well try to get a few holes in. I heard there was a dynamite course around here somewhere. What's your handicap?"

"About a twenty," I replied.

"Well, coach, we've got plenty of time to try and improve your golf swing," he said with a laugh, "and try to find you some decent clothes to wear."

We discovered the most immaculate eighteen-hole course. It reminded me a lot of Augusta National with its majestic dogwood trees, azaleas, monstrous snow-white sand traps, and slick greens. The tee markers were made of solid gold, and they issued us diamond-studded golf clubs. Some youngsters with wings stood by just in case we needed a caddie. I'm sure golfers around the world had wondered if they'd get to play the game in eternity. Well, the answer is yes, at least for some of us. For others, it might be just a little too hot to play. That's a joke.

Johnny disappeared into the magnificent clubhouse that looked a lot like the White House. He reappeared moments later dressed in cardinal-and-gold golf knickers with a gold shirt, cardinal pants, gold socks, and brilliant white golf shoes. He looked stunning.

"Coach," he said with a voice of disappointment. "I couldn't get any knickers for you. They said you hadn't qualified yet."

I wondered what he meant by that as we headed to the first tee.

Johnny smoked his drive on the first hole. He knocked the ball about 270 yards right down the middle. If he hadn't been a college basketball coach, he could have certainly been a professional golfer on the PGA tour. He was that good.

As usual, I hooked my drive about 230 yards into the rough. I wasn't making excuses but it was the first time I ever played golf in a hospital gown. Johnny parred the first hole, and I double-bo-geyed. We arrived at the tee on the second hole, a par three, and were stunned to see who waited to tee off. In all their glory stood Bob Hope, who died in 2003; Jack Benny, who passed in 1974; Ben Hogan, who passed away in 1997; and Payne Stewart, who died trag-ically in 1999, all dressed in colorful knickers. I stared at them in disbelief.

Mr. Hope looked at me and smiled.

"Son, I should have taken you with me on my USO shows tour in Vietnam. You would have knocked them dead wearing that outfit."

They all roared with laughter.

I almost died from embarrassment, and we all had a big laugh, with Johnny's laugh sounding the loudest.

This eternity is really not a bad place to be, I thought.

Our round of golf went great, and I couldn't believe the com-pany I was with. When we finished, Johnny came up to me and grasped my hand. "That was fun, wasn't it, coach? But I'd give any-thing to go back and coach the Cyclones at Hilton Coliseum," he said with a forlorn look.

He pulled me closer and I could see the tears in his eyes.

"Why didn't they want to give me any golf clothes, John?" I asked.

"I guess they considered you only a visitor, coach," he replied.

"Am I not dead, coach?" I asked.

"I can't say one way or the other, coach," he said. "But if you aren't, go back to your life on earth and enjoy and savor every minute of it. I would give anything to go back and coach and enjoy Thanksgiving and Christmas and take lots of walks and hug and kiss my dear wife and family again."

He gave me one last long hug.

"Goodbye, coach," he said and turned and walked slowly back toward the clubhouse.

Am I really dead, I thought, *or was the Almighty just giving me a tour of what to expect?*

CHAPTER 4

Audie Murphy

I stopped dead in my tracks when I saw Medal of Honor winner and iconic actor, Audie Murphy. He had lost his life at age forty-five on May 28, 1971, in a plane crash in Brush Mountain, Virginia. He wasn't a very tall person, about five feet five inches tall, and no more than a hundred fifty to a hundred sixty pounds. He had thick black hair and a handsome face, and he wore an old World War II green Army jacket. He was hardly the image of one of our fiercest soldiers in combat. What was noticeable were all the medals pinned on the front of his jacket. Every Army service medal you could imagine. I think I counted about thirty including the Medal of Honor, two Silver Stars, two Bronze Stars, and three Purple Hearts.

"Mr. Murphy, I'm a huge fan of yours," I called out. "I watched all your Western movies and I really enjoyed you in *Night Passage* with Jimmy Stewart. I thought you were great as the Silver Kid in *The Duel at Silver Creek* with Steven McNally and a young Lee Marvin. You were delightful in *The Guns At Fort Petticoat* saving all those women. I've seen all your movies, I bet."

He stopped and turned toward me and gave me quite a quizzical look like *who is this person dressed in hospital garb?* He then thrust out his hand for me to shake. "Call me Audie," he said with that famous Hollywood smile.

"I'm also a combat and Purple Heart veteran like you, sir," I said.

"Don't call me sir, I'm not an Army officer anymore," he said with a Hollywood smirk. "What war were you in?"

"Vietnam, sir, I mean Audie," I replied. "I'm sorry you lost your life. You were such a great soldier and actor. I think I watched every movie you made, even *To Hell and Back*. How did you manage to kill so many Germans in World War II and survive?"

The look on his face turned serious and penetrating.

"It's funny that you ask that," he said. "Did I catch your name?"

"Oh, I'm sorry I didn't introduce myself properly, Audie. I'm Tony Powers from West Des Moines, Iowa. I was a sportscaster in life and I think I died on the operating table. As you can see, I didn't even have a chance to change clothes."

"I noticed that," he said, glancing up and down at my hospital garb. "In answer to your question, isn't it ironic that I should have been killed many times in World War II only to die in a plane crash? Yes, I helped kill a lot of Germans and I saw many of our guys get killed. Even though I was a successful movie star, I suffered terribly with PTSD. If you're a decent human being, you never forget all that death and combat. When I reach the end of the line here, God will judge me on that. What year did you die?"

"In 2014," I replied.

A look of exasperation flashed across the actor's face.

"You mean I've been up here forty-nine years and still have not been judged? I think the Good Lord has punished me already. You must have survived Vietnam," he said.

Together we surveyed the long lines of people moving ever so slowly toward the brilliant, illimunated clouds in the distance.

"Yes, Audie, I survived the Vietnam War but, like you, it haunted me the rest of my life. I suffered terribly from PTSD with the nightmares and night sweats. I killed and should have been killed. God will judge me too. You wouldn't have known about the conflicts in the Middle East Gulf War, the war in Iraq, Kuwait, and Afganistan in the 1990s and early 2000s. We lost many brave soldiers fighting regimes and terrorists in those countries. Many veterans lost limbs to IEDs, improvised explosive devices. Terrorists attacked the New

York City Twin Towers on September 11, 2001, and killed over three thousand brave Americans."

An astonished look appeared on Audie's face.

"Oh my god," he exclaimed. "They attacked our own country and buildings in New York City?"

"Yes, a terrorist named Osama Bin Laden devised a plan for terrorists to train as pilots, hijack U.S. airliners, and then fly them into the World Trade Center Twin Towers, the Pentagon, and the White House. The plane that targeted the White House crashed because some brave passengers intervened and fought the hijackers before the plane could reach the White House. We later hunted down all the people responsible. They were called the Taliban and were in Afghanistan. We defeated them, Audie, just like you did to the Germans in World War II," I said proudly.

"Wow, I've missed a lot," he said. "I died while we were still fighting in Vietnam. Did we win that war?"

"Well, Audie," I said, "the Vietnam War didn't officially end until 1975. People said we lost the war, but I didn't agree. We only lost the will to fight. Over fifty eight thousand brave Americans gave up their lives in that war. They're all up here with us walking the road to judgment."

While I talked, Audie kept glancing over his shoulder at the throngs of folks who walked by.

I didn't want to bother the famous actor any longer. I knew he wanted to continue his march to judgment day.

"I don't want to keep you, Audie. It's been a real thrill for me to have visited with you. I commend you for your military service and acting career. You were a great American hero."

"Tony, it's been a pleasure," he said gently shaking my hand. "Hopefully we'll meet again in eternity. Thank you for the history lesson and your service. I had a magnificent war hero life and I would give anything to do it again. I miss my wife and kids and all those actors and actresses I knew in Hollywood. You're right, Tony, I should have died in World War II rather than in a plane crash."

He turned around and disappeared into the sea of people all walking toward judgment day.

28

I felt excited and exhilarated. I had just met the most famous World War II hero in history and one of the most iconic actors of our time. We had had a deep and involved conversation that I will never forget.

CHAPTER 5

Jim Duncan

I rubbed my eyes in disbelief when I spotted Jim Duncan, the late voice of the Drake Relays. I almost missed him when he trudged by me in the huge procession of people on the way to judgment. He wore a light-blue blazer over a white pullover shirt with dark blue pants and had a white cap with the inscription "Drake Relays" on the front. His shoes were so white they glowed, and he wore pale-blue socks and a gold whistle hung around his neck. He had the Drake colors bestowed all over him.

"Hey, Jim Duncan, voice of the Drake Relays," I called out.

He stopped, turned, and eyed me with two huge eyeballs magnified by the lenses in his glasses. He was nearly bent over from osteoporosis. There was a glint of recognition in his stare.

"Tony, what in heaven's name are you doing here?" he asked.

I was thrilled when this icon recognized me and thrust my right hand out to shake his.

"It's been a long time and many relays ago, Jim, that you passed away. Did you know they remodeled Drake Stadium and renamed the field after Bulldogs football legend Johnny Bright? And the blue oval track, Jim, they named after you, my friend. It's now called Jim Duncan Truck."

A pleased look came over his face and he smiled.

"You don't say, Tony. The same stadium named after the great Johnny Bright and me? I'm happy they remembered me, but those things don't really matter up here."

He turned and stared toward the throngs of people as they walked toward judgment day.

"I'm sure when I get up there the Lord won't care what was named after me on earth. He'll want to know what good I did for mankind, Tony. I lived on earth a long time, but I'm going to be up here a heck of a lot longer. I hope the Good Lord looks past my iniquities."

He stared at me again with big, dark-blue eyes.

"How'd you get up here, Tony? I bet you had a good life."

"Well, Jimmy, I had my left knee scoped but never woke up after the surgery. Yes, I had a wonderful life. I did everything except win the lottery."

He bowled over with laughter.

"That won't do you a bit of good up here, Tony."

"Jim, you were irreplaceable as the voice of the Drake Relays. I remember how you extolled the fans on both sides of the stadium to get on their feet and cheer for the runners. Many records were set because of your enthusiasm, Jimmy. Your voice would boom out of the microphone, 'Okay, fans on the east side, we're on record pace. Let's bring them home. Get on your feet and let's help set another record. Here they come, fans on the west side, get on your feet too and help bring them to the finish line.' You'd have eighteen thousand fans cheering them on, Jim."

"Everybody's replaceable, Tony. I just loved to fire up the crowd."

"What was your greatest Drake Relays moment, Jim?"

"Oh gosh, Tony, there were many. But I got goose bumps when Olympian Steve Scott ran the fastest fifteen hundred meters in Drake history in 3:38.27 back in 1984, which was pretty sweet."

He looked back at the mass of humanity that made its way up toward the giant cloud in the distance, then stared back at me.

I could tell he wanted to end our visit and be on his way. I didn't blame him. There were more important things ahead.

He thrust out his hand, and I noticed the Drake Relays watch on his wrist, a real collector's item now.

"I suppose I need to get back in line, Tony. I'm not a young man anymore. I was seventy-eight when I died in 1989 and I've got a long ways to go before these ancient legs of mine give out. Good luck to you when you finally get to the top. All the records in the world won't help any of us now."

I felt a tinge of regret as I shook hands with this Drake icon.

I watched him as he struggled to find his place again in the line. He walked slightly bent over like there was a huge weight on his back. He soon disappeared from sight. There had to be a special place for him ahead, I thought. He was a great credit to the world and to mankind. Drake alumni revered him all across the country when he was alive.

"Goodbye, Jim," I whispered to myself.

CHAPTER 6

Doreen Wilber

I tried to remember when I last interviewed Doreen Wilber, the world champion archer from Jefferson, Iowa, who won a gold medal in the 1972 Munich Olympic Games. I believed it was around 1974. I was very surprised when I noticed her off to the side of the road to judgment shooting some target arrows. It had to be her, I thought. She wore a red shirt with white and blue stars with the words *USA Archery* inscribed on the back. An Olympic gold medal hung from her neck. It had a brilliant, yellowish glow.

She wore dark-rimmed glasses, and each arrow she shot was dead on target. The clincher for me was the inscription on her duffel bag that said *Property of Doreen Wilber, Jefferson, Iowa*. She had passed away in 2008 at the age of seventy-eight but didn't look a day over fifty. She not only was a world-class archer in her lifetime but a world-class cook as well.

"You've got to be Doreen Wilber," I said. "Nobody can shoot an arrow dead center like that and bake an apple pie like you did."

She turned and gazed at me through her glasses and studied me for a moment. I could tell she wondered who I was and why I wore a hospital gown.

"You kind of look vaguely familiar," she said. "Do I know you?"

"It's been about forty years since I interviewed you in your backyard in Jefferson, Iowa, as a young sports reporter for WHO-TV in Des Moines," I replied. "Then you treated me to a couple of pieces of the best apple pie that I ever ate. It literally melted in my mouth, it was so good. I think you also added a scoop or two of homemade ice cream. Man oh man, was I in food heaven."

She chuckled.

"Now I remember you. You're Tony Powers and you worked with Jim Zabel. That was a nice feature of me you ran on television back then. Everybody in Jefferson saw it. You also said I should have won a gold medal in pie making. I'm glad you liked my pie, but I don't think you've quite made it to heaven just yet. How did you get here in that outfit?" she said as she eyed my green gown.

"I had arthroscopic knee surgery for a slightly torn meniscus. When they put me under, I never woke up. I passed away right on the operating table. It happens every day. I guess when your time is up, it's up."

"The hospital should have dressed you up in a tuxedo before the surgery then," she laughed. "You want to shoot a few arrows?"

"You bet," I answered. "I've already played catch with Nile Kinnick and golfed with Johnny Orr up here."

She looked at me with a quizzical expression and handed me a bow and arrow.

"You threw a football around with the great Nile Kinnick?" she asked in a disbelieving tone. "Is Johnny around here too?"

"Yes, Nile's a wonderful person. We had a great time heaving the pigskin around. Johnny and I played eighteen holes on the most beautiful golf course you could ever imagine. Little angels flew around ready to caddie. We had diamond-studded golf clubs, and the tee markers were made of solid gold. You wouldn't believe who played in a foursome right in front of us. No other than Bob Hope, Jack Benny, Ben Hogan, and Payne Stewart."

She stared at me with a dubious look and shook her head.

"It sounds like you had the time of your life here and you haven't even been to judgment day yet," she said. "Is that possible?"

"Well, maybe the Good Lord is giving me sort of a reprieve before he finally calls me home," I said. "I've got no complaints. Let's see what I can do with this bow and arrow."

It took almost all my strength to pull the arrow back and let it go. It flew twenty feet over the target.

She giggled at my ineptness.

"What year did you leave earth?" she asked and handed me another arrow.

"Very recently," I answered. "In 2014. What was it like to have won that gold medal in Munich and all the tragedy that surrounded the 1972 Olympics?"

"Oh, having won the gold medal changed my life for the better," she said. "But I felt so bad for the Israeli wrestlers who were killed by the terrorists. I still remember the words of sportscaster Jim McKay, who said, 'They're gone. They're all gone.' It was absolutely terrible. I had a great life on the national stage and in Jefferson, Tony. I'm so happy you loved my pies. So did many others. Gosh, I've been gone six years and am still waiting for judgment. I guess I'd better get back in line."

I fired off the last arrow she'd handed me, and it flew thirty feet over the target.

She laughed heartily and packed up her duffel bag and slung it over her shoulder.

"So long, Tony. I hope the Lord gives you a fair shake at the end. Heaven knows you can't shoot an arrow very well."

"So long to you, Doreen, and thank you for that great pie."

I watched her get back into the procession and then vanish.

A housewife from Jefferson, Iowa, who won an Olympic gold medal in archery.

Absolutely incredible, I thought.

CHAPTER 7

Ronald Reagan

I almost fainted—how could I faint if I'm already dead?—when I spotted President Ronald Reagan, the fortieth President of the United States on the road to judgment. He looked very commanding and presidential in a dark suit and red tie. His brown hair was neatly combed, and he didn't look a day over sixty. He had died in 2004 at the age of ninety-three. People seemed to grow younger than older in eternity, and President Reagan was one of them. Were we in some kind of time warp? I wondered.

I knew just what to say to get his attention.

"WHO, Mr. President."

He stopped maybe three feet from me. He had his famous dog Lucky at his side, a giant Bouvier des Flandres the size of a pony. They both gawked at me.

"Did I hear you say WHO, young man? Did you mean WHO Radio?" he said.

I was in such awe I could hardly answer him.

"Yes, sir, Mr. President," I finally blurted out. "Tony Powers is my name. I mean it was my name in real life and I worked for WHO Radio too with Jim Zabel."

A giant smile broke across his face and he stuck out his hand to shake mine. He had a very firm grip.

"Wellllll," he replied. "Glad to meet you, Tony. Any friend and employee of WHO Radio and Jim Zabel is a friend of Lucky and mine. I loved doing play-by-play for the Chicago Cubs on WHO. I sat in the studio in Des Moines and did the games live via ticker tape from Wrigley Field. I had to do quite a bit of adlibbing in those days." He laughed. Lucky barked, like he knew what the president had said. Mr. Reagan threw his head back and roared with that trademark Reagan laugh.

"This dog was smarter than most members of Congress were when I was president, Tony," he said.

We had a good chuckle at that one.

"I thought you were one of our greatest presidents, Mr. President," I said. "I always remembered your famous quote when you challenged the Russian leadership to tear down and end the Berlin Wall: 'Mr. Gorbachev, tear down this wall!'"

"Thank you for the compliment, Anthony, and I hope God thinks I did a good job too. My wife Nancy and I tried to live our lives as good, decent, and churchgoing citizens. When she finally joins us up here, we're going to be judged one of these days, and we hope the Good Lord looks past all our failures. God knows there were plenty of them while we were alive."

He eyed my green hospital gown.

"Did something happen to you in the hospital, Tony?" he asked. "It looks like your life was cut short far too soon."

"Yes, sir, Mr. President. I injured my knee working out at the local YMCA. I went in for minor knee surgery. They put me under, and I never woke up again. But I had an outstanding life, no regrets. I worked for WHO Radio and did play-by-play for Iowa, Iowa State, and Drake. I've had a great time so far up here. I've even met the legendary Nile Kinnick, and now to meet you and your dog in person is just unbelievable. I could spend the rest of my eternity just meeting famous people like you, but I know I'll be judged someday soon. Can I ask you about the time the ticker tape machine quit working at WHO while you were doing a Cubs game?"

He looked down at Lucky and smiled. I could tell the great storyteller was ready to tell a story.

"Wellllll," he said. "In those days, the ticker tape just told you the basics like *he hit a foul ball into the seats* or *he singled into right field*. The announcer had to fill in the rest. I remember one game when the Cubs hitter was at the plate and fouled off the first pitch into the bleachers. Well, just then the ticker tape went dead. I proceeded to call about ten straight pitches, and they all were fouled back into the seats. Then the ticker tape came back to life. The Cubs hitter singled to left field, and I breathed a sigh of relief," he reminisced with a smile.

I noticed Lucky as he tugged at the president's arm, signaling for them to get going on the road to judgment.

I wouldn't delay them any longer.

"It's been a real pleasure to have met you, Mr. President, and Lucky," I said. "Long live WHO Radio."

We shook hands, and President Reagan slipped something into my hand. I watched them until they disappeared into the mass of humanity on the road back to judgment day. A man and his faithful dog as they walked into eternity together. I was almost moved to tears because I had been so proud to have met one of my predecessors at WHO Radio. He'd be remembered forever as a world, national, and Iowa icon. I opened my hand and stared at what he'd shoved into it. It was something I would cherish forever.

There were three jelly beans. One was red, one was white, and the other was blue.

CHAPTER 8

Bill Reichardt

I didn't know how long I had walked toward judgment day when I spotted another familiar face on the road. He was dressed in a patented Reichardt's clothing store gray pinstriped suit and looked impeccable in a blue shirt with a button-down collar and with a black-and-gold Southwick tie. His feet were adorned with shiny black wing tip shoes. It could be nobody else, I thought. It was the legendary Bill Reichardt who had passed away in 2004 just shy of his seventy-fourth birthday.

"I'm Bill Reichardt and I own the store," I kiddingly said to him as I recalled the famous television commercial he was known for.

He stopped, turned his head, and stared at me for a long second. Then he eyed my hospital gown, shook his head, and laughed.

"Tony, I thought I taught you how to dress better. We'll have to find you a new tailor. What in God's holy name are you doing here?"

"Hi, Bill," I said. "What a surprise to run into you up here. I really enjoyed wearing your suits on earth. I wish I could have brought one with me. You see, I died pretty quick in the hospital—I didn't wake up after knee surgery—and they didn't have any Reichardt suits for me to wear in the hereafter."

He smiled and I could see that he appreciated the compliment.

"What year is it?" he asked.

"It's 2014, Bill."

He looked confused.

"You mean I've been on this darn road for ten years and I still haven't got to the top? It seemed like only yesterday that I passed away. Does time stand still up here, you think?" he asked.

"I guess so. We're in eternity, Bill. There is really no time but God's time. You died a real sports legend in Iowa, and folks will always remember your television commercials where you said, 'No sale is ever final here because I'm here. I'm Bill Reichardt and I own the store.' Jim Zabel and I loved to wear your suits when we announced the sports on WHO-TV newscasts. We always wondered how you became an all-American fullback at Iowa and the Big Ten's MVP in 1951 by not winning a single conference game."

A gargantuan smile spread across his face when I mentioned Iowa football.

"That crazy Zabel should have known, Tony, he did the play-by-play," he laughed. "You know me, Tony. Even though we weren't very good, I fought hard for every yard. I didn't quit. I played the game the way it should have been played, very physical. Just like in the clothing business, you have to dress successful to be successful. God gave me the ability to play football, and that is the way my whole life was. I tried to be a success in everything I tried, from football to clothing to politics to handball to family.

"I founded the Little All-American Football League to try to make kids successful, and I hope the Good Lord gives me a little credit for that. We helped turn a lot of kids' lives around on the football field. Football builds discipline, and discipline builds fortitude and respect. God gave me extraordinary talent on the football field and in life."

"You were an Iowa sports icon on the field and off, Bill. What a career you had. Drafted by the Green Bay Packers, you played one year in the NFL. Then you opened a very successful clothing store and even ran for the state legislature and governor."

"Thank you for the compliments, Tony. It means a lot coming from you. I wish I had come along a little later in my playing days, though. That way I could have played for those legendary coaches Forest Evasheski at Iowa and maybe Vince Lombardi for the Green Bay Packers. But that's how life played out for me. The only thing that counts now is how I performed in life. I don't think God will care whether I played for Evasheski or Lombardi or was the Big Ten's most valuable player in 1951."

"I remembered you as a pretty good handball player, Bill. Remember that bet we made years ago, that if I scored a point against you in handball, you'd give me one of your suits free? You won the bet," I said.

He laughed out loud.

"Yes, I remember it well. As I recall, you trained with Chuck Housman, one of the all-time handball greats at the Des Moines downtown riverfront YMCA. For a novice, you weren't bad, but I wasn't about to let you score a point on me and get a five-hundred-dollar suit for nothing. I practiced hard for a couple of weeks to get ready for you," he said with a chuckle.

"Bill, we still wouldn't have had an Iowa State, Iowa, football game each year without you. The teams wouldn't play each other, and you had to sponsor a bill when you were in the Iowa legislature to get them to play each other again. It's been a whale of a series ever since."

"It's fantastic for the state of Iowa to play the game each season, Tony. It's one of college football's top rivalries, and I'm happy that it's played each year now. I hope they never end it."

"As I recall, Bill, you were quite opinionated on a number of topics, including football."

"I see you must have heard and read my editorials on television and in the newspaper," he said with a smirk. "Yes, I had an opinion on just about everything. But all that is in the past now. The only opinion that counts now is the Good Lord's. I had a super life, Tony, and hope you had one too. I certainly had my faults, and I hope God overlooked them. I heard he's very forgiving."

He turned and stared at the huge throng of folks making their way to judgment day.

"Ditto that, Bill," I said. "I see you want to get back on that road so I won't keep you much longer. Guess who I've seen already up here?"

"Who?"

"Well, there's been Nile Kinnick, Johnny Orr, John Wayne, Jimmy Stewart, Audie Murphy, Jim Duncan, Bob Hope, Joan Rivers, Napoleon, and Einstein, to name a few."

He had an astounded look on his face.

"You saw the great Nile Kinnick?"

"We threw the football around in a place that looked like the Garden of Eden. We visited and talked about his Heisman Trophy. What a super guy. I even played golf with Johnny Orr up here."

"Johnny's here too?"

"The one and only and in all his glory," I said with a smile.

He stared at me in a long moment of disbelief. Then he looked again toward the heavens where the mammoth procession seemed to never end. He turned back around and looked deep into my eyes.

"Are you sure you're really dead, Tony? You've had a great time up here. I haven't noticed any of those folks here. I guess I've spent all my time just trying to get up there. Maybe I should slow down a little and enjoy the trip like you."

"You have to look for them, Bill. They're all up here, even Jim Zabel somewhere."

"Please do me one favor before you leave, Tony."

"What's that, Bill?"

"Find some new clothes, preferably a Reichardt's or Mr. B's suit."

We both laughed and shook hands, and he got back into the line. I watched him until the pinstripes on his suit seemed to vanish in the distance.

I hope he really bumps into Nile Kinnick, I thought. *Boy, would they have a great time together.*

CHAPTER 9

Johnny Bright

I got back into line and again started my long march. I'd estimated I had walked several days, or it could have been several years—in eternity everything seemed timeless—when I heard some wonderful singing just behind me. They sang, "O when the saints go marching in, I want to be in that number when the saints go marching in." I stopped and turned around to watch a chorus group of around twenty souls. Most were dressed in dazzling blue robes and red scarves, but my eye caught a glimpse of an athletic and handsome African American man who stood out from the group. He wore a blue sweater with a big white "D" on the front, immaculate white pants, and white shoes.

He came closer, and I recognized him from his pictures in the newspapers. *Wow, this was getting interesting*, I thought.

The man was Drake's iconic football all-American, Johnny Bright. He had died in 1983 at the still young age of fifty-three. He looked much younger and, man, could he sing. His deep voice belted out the song and he sounded just like the legendary Iowa opera singer Simon Estes.

I had to make a decision to either call out to him or let him pass by. I decided to get his attention.

"Drake football," I shouted as he started to pass by me.

He stopped singing and immediately approached me with his right hand extended. His chorus group kept chugging along. "O

43

when the saints, O when the saints, O when the saints go marching in," they sang.

"I'm Johnny Bright," he said as we shook hands. "I loved playing football for Drake. Were you a Bulldogs fan?"

I was struck spellbound. Here stood the great Johnny Bright with great big eyes and a neatly trimmed mustache. He looked like he could still play.

"I'm Tony Powers, Mr. Bright. I didn't mean to interrupt your wonderful singing. Your chorus group is getting away," I said.

"Oh, don't worry about that. I'll catch up to them. I'm still fast in my old age," he said with a laugh. "You can call me Johnny."

"I'd heard so much about you," I said excitedly. "I was only a young child when you played for Drake in the 1950s and became an all-American. I covered Drake football as a sportscaster for WHO-TV in Des Moines in the 1980s. Chuck Shelton was the coach back then, and Drake upset Colorado and Iowa State in those years. But they always talked about you, Johnny. They renamed the football field at Drake Stadium Johnny Bright Field, and you were named the greatest football player in Drake history."

His eyes grew misty at the news and he became a little emotional.

"I've been dead a long time, Tony. Thank you for letting me know. But I'm not sure It will help me when I reach judgment day whether they named Drake's football field after me. It's how I lived my life that will count, not how many yards I rushed for or touchdowns I scored. It's all going to come down on how I played the game of life."

He stared a moment at my hospital clothes.

"Did you have a good life, Tony? I don't mean to pry but it looked like you never made it out of the hospital."

"I went in for torn meniscus surgery, Johnny, that's all, and I didn't wake up afterward. I must have gone into cardiac arrest and they couldn't bring me back. But I did have a great life, Johnny. No complaints."

I wanted terribly to ask him about Wilbanks Smith and the broken jaw incident in 1951 and the famous photo that won the Pulitzer Prize.

He seemed to have read my mind.

"That's great, Tony. I mean it wasn't great that you died but that you had a great life. I've forgiven all my enemies, even Wilbanks Smith, who broke my jaw back in 1951 when we played Oklahoma A&M. There was a lot of racism in those days, and African American athletes like myself were targets. But you had to forgive and forget. Even after my broken jaw at Drake, I still played twelve seasons in the Canadian Football League for the Calgary Stampeders and the Edmonton Eskimos and became the CFL's all-time leading rusher. I was blessed with a fine career, Tony, despite all the hate."

"That photo in the *Des Moines Register* made you famous, Johnny. As you know, it ended up shown in every major newspaper in the country. It looked so vicious and violent."

"I ended up drinking milkshakes for a couple of months afterward, but it really didn't affect my playing career that much. If I were to meet Mr. Smith right now, I would shake his hand. You can't hold any grievances up here, Tony. You have to let it all go. When I finally face God, I want my life's slate to be wiped free with no blemishes. He gave me a great life. I wish I could have lived a little while longer, but it wasn't to be. I died in 1983. Do you know what year it is now, Tony?"

"Well, I think it's around 2014. That's the year I died, but you can never tell up here. It could be 2050 and I wouldn't know it. Time doesn't seem to exist here. Did you ever hear the name Jack Trice, Johnny?"

He looked perplexed for a moment.

"I don't believe I have," he answered.

"He died in 1923 at the age of twenty-one and was the first African American athlete to play football for Iowa State. They named Iowa State's football stadium after him. He passed away from internal injuries after Iowa State played Minnesota. Some believed he was deliberately targeted by Minnesota players and he was fatally injured after they piled on him after a play."

"Really," he said. "I'd love to meet him and congratulate him. Football can be a dangerous game, Tony. A lot of bad things can happen to you. I sure hope they didn't intentionally do it. They'd have to answer to the Good Lord then. Wow, Johnny Bright Field and Jake Trice Stadium. I'm sure glad they remembered us."

Our conversation was interrupted by beautiful singing. The chorus group had made a U-turn and had returned to find Johnny. They weren't going to leave him behind.

"C'mon and join us awhile, Tony," he invited me. "You've got the time, don't you?" He laughed.

"I've got all the time in the world," I replied.

Even though I wasn't quite dressed to be marching with the sharp-looking chorus, we rejoined the group and started singing, "I want to be in that number when the saints go marching in."

I felt exhilarated and extremely happy as I belted out the tunes.

I couldn't think of a better way to march some of the way to judgment day alongside the iconic Johnny Bright as a singing partner.

He still looked like a great athlete. As we marched and sang, I thought more about the "Johnny Bright Incident." It took Drake University years to finally receive an official apology from Oklahoma A&M, now Oklahoma State University, for the cheap-shot injury to Bright. I was gratified at how he forgave his attacker and all those racial injustices he endured during his career.

What a class act, I thought.

CHAPTER 10

John Wooden

I had never forgotten my trip to UCLA's Pauley Pavilion in the West Regional of the 1988 NCAA basketball tournament. My assignment for WHO-TV was to cover head coach Tom Davis and the Iowa Hawkeyes as they battled Florida State in the first round. The Hawks won a thriller and faced mighty Louisville in the second round.

After the game, I had walked around the corner of Pauley Pavilion and almost bumped into an elderly gentleman going the other way. I excused myself and was startled to see who I had almost run into. It was the "Wizard of Westwood," the legendary UCLA coach and icon John Wooden. He had coached the Bruins for twenty-seven seasons and won ten national titles. I had introduced myself, and we proceeded to have a fifteen-minute conversation on the Hawkeyes' performance and about coach Davis. Coach Wooden was very impressed with the Iowa program.

That's why I was particularly excited to have noticed him again on the road to judgment. He lived almost a century when he passed away in 2010 at age ninety-nine. He still looked like a basketball coach. He wore a gold-colored sweatshirt with blue lettering that said *Property of UCLA Basketball.* A blue whistle hung around his neck, and he carried a clipboard that had diagrammed basketball plays on it. He didn't look a day over sixty-nine with his short, silver-whitish hair. He seemed ready to coach forever.

"Coach Wooden," I said. "Excuse me, sir, I met you some years back at the 1988 West Regional in Los Angeles. We discussed the Iowa Hawkeyes and coach Tom Davis. You loved the Iowa Hawkeye team. My name is Tony Powers. I was a sports reporter for WHO-TV in Des Moines back then."

He stopped walking and looked me dead in the eye. His look seemed to penetrate right through me. Then he smiled.

"Tom Davis was a brilliant coach," he said. "As I recall, the Hawkeyes won that regional and then played Arizona in the West Regional semifinals in Seattle."

I was amazed at his tremendous memory and the ability to remember games played nearly thirty years ago.

"That's right, sir. The Hawkeyes beat Florida State and Louisville then lost to Arizona. Arizona went on to the Final Four that year."

"You're correct," he said. "You've got a good memory. You said you're from Iowa. Johnny Orr was a pretty fair coach at Iowa State then. That Jeff Hornacek was a tremendous player for him."

"I met Johnny up here, and we even played a round of golf."

Even the Wizard of Westwood looked surprised.

"Hey, you must have had some pull with God to have done that, Tony," he said laughing.

"I still can't believe it myself, coach," I replied. "Boy, would he have loved to see you. Coach, remember that Drake team you played in the 1969 Final Four?"

He thought for a second, then responded with a huge smile.

"Now you're going way back, Tony," he said. "You bet I do. I can even recall the score. We barely won eighty-five to eighty-two. They had some guys named Dolph Pulliam and Willie Wise who really took it to us. We were very fortunate to win."

The coach then turned and looked back at the long procession of souls that trudged along the road to judgment.

"I know it sounds like a cliché, Tony, but we've got one more big game to play yet," he said. "Did you live your life well?"

"I think so, coach. But the Good Lord will decide that. You know, we can reminisce about all those great games but they are really only games. Who won and who lost doesn't mean a great deal up here. Sure, I did some things in life I regret, and I hope God forgives me. There were times when I just didn't use my God-given talents the way they should have been used. It's funny, coach. We save these nest eggs to spend in our retirement, but money doesn't do us a bit of good here in eternity. You're better off giving it all to the less fortunate."

"Amen, Tony," he said. "Well spoken. The Lord gave me ninety-nine years on earth and all those championship teams and coach of the year honors. The awards don't mean anything up here. I think I helped develop good citizens and Christians, and I think I gave back a lot to the community and the world. I'm ready to move on now and face my judgment."

He stuck out his hand and vigorously shook my hand.

"It's been a pleasure to meet you, Tony. Good luck up there."

"Good luck to you, coach," I said.

He turned and moved slowly back into line and soon disappeared from my sight.

There's got to be a special place waiting for him, I thought.

CHAPTER 11

Alex Karras

I continued to recognize familiar faces on the road to judgment day. I saw actors and actresses like Alan Ladd, who died in 1964; Tyrone Power, who passed in 1958; Grace Kelly, who passed on after a traffic accident in 1982; and famous people like Princess Diana, who died tragically in 1997, and General George Patton, who passed in 1945. Ladd, Power, and Kelly were all dressed like they were about to attend the latest Hollywood Academy Awards. Both men wore dark suits with black ties, and Ms. Kelly looked absolutely stunning in a blue dress. They were dressed in their Sunday best to see the Lord, I thought, and quite a contrast from the way I was dressed in a green hospital gown.

Princess Di looked immaculate in a pink gown, and General Patton's three stars glistened on his greenish-brown U.S. Army uniform. His famed white bull terrier, Willie, walked by his side. I didn't think God would care what clothes we wore on judgment day. He'd look deep into our souls and pronounce judgment. That was fine with me. It bothered me when I saw a parent who carried a newborn infant or a young child as they walked by on the road to judgment. It didn't seem fair to me that their lives had been shortened by accidents, illnesses, or wars when I had lived a long, full life. But I knew God had a plan for everyone.

I noticed a big man approaching. He wore a black Iowa Hawkeye letterman's jacket with a big gold "I" emblazoned on the front. He had short, black hair and a mustache. He walked like he was in a hurry and stared straight ahead. He was probably around six feet three inches tall and weighed about 250 pounds. He wore tinted glasses and looked quite intimidating, like a bouncer.

Then I recognized him.

It was former Iowa Hawkeye and Detroit Lions football great Alex Karras. He'd passed away in 2012 at the age of seventy-seven, but he looked forty-seven. He was also known as Mondo, of *Blazing Saddles* movie fame, and George Papadopoulos from the hit television show *Webster*.

I would have loved to have interviewed him in my sportscasting career. This was my chance. I had to think of a way to get his attention. What could I say that would get this television and movie star to stop? I got it, I thought.

"Could I get your autograph, Mr. Karras?" I cried out.

Like a slowing freight train, his pace slowed to a crawl, then he stopped and stared at me with huge dark eyes behind the tinted glasses. At first he had an annoyed look then a slight grin appeared on his face.

"Gee whiz, fella," he said. "We can't sign any autographs up here. Don't you know we're all equal up here and there shouldn't be any celebrities? If anything, I should have asked for your autograph. We're on the road to judgment and it just wouldn't look right for a person to sign autographs here. The Lord said, 'The first shall be last and the last shall be first.' We're all very humble and on equal footing here."

"I understand, sir," I said. "I just wanted to get your attention. I'm Tony Powers and I covered Iowa football in the 1970s and 1980s for WHO-TV in Des Moines. I worked with Jim Zabel for sixteen years. I see you're still proud to wear your Iowa letterman's jacket."

A look of satisfaction crossed his face.

"You don't have to call me sir either. My name's Alex, and contrary to what some in the media thought, that I hated Coach Evy (Forest Evashevski), I thoroughly enjoyed my football days at Iowa. If there were any ill feelings between me and the coach, I've left all that behind me. If I met him up here, I'd give him a giant bear hug and tell him I loved him. We shouldn't judge anyone up here. The Lord said, 'Judge not lest ye be judged.' What happened to you, Tony? It appears you didn't make it out of the hospital," he said.

"Minor knee surgery gone bad, Alex. They fixed a minor meniscus tear, but I never woke up afterward."

"Bummer," he said. "You look like you still had some years to go before coming up here. My body just wore out."

"Can I ask you a silly question, Alex?"

"Sure."

"Did you ever get a chance to pull Howard Cosell's hairpiece off when you were on Monday Night Football?"

He let out a laugh that sounded like a bull moose bellowing.

"Oh heavens no," he laughed. "The only guys who tried that were Muhammed Ali and Dandy Don Meredith. I really enjoyed working with Howard."

"What do you remember most about your playing days at Iowa?" I asked. "Your quarterback was my friend, the great Randy Duncan."

"You knew Randy? He was a fantastic quarterback and should have won the Heisman Trophy. Sure, Coach Evy and I had some major run-ins. You had to play both ways in those days in the 1950s, contrary to today's game. I loved defensive tackle but hated offense. My most memorable game was when we beat Notre Dame forty-eight to eight to close out the 1956 season. I grew up in Indiana, and everybody wanted to beat the Irish in those days. Then we went on and beat Oregon State in the 1957 Rose Bowl. That was pretty sweet."

"You were named a first team all-American and drafted by the Detroit Lions. You were probably the best defensive tackle in the NFL in the 1960s but never made it into the NFL's Hall of Fame. Didn't that ever bother you?" I asked.

He stared at me a moment and let out a breath of air.

"I suppose you had to ask that question, Tony," he said. "I'd be lying if I said it hadn't mattered. They had their reasons for not inducting me. But it doesn't really make any difference up here, does it? I'm going to see the Good Lord on judgment day, and I'm sure he's not going to care whether my bronze bust is in Canton, Ohio, or not. I sure hope he loved football, though."

"I thought your wife, Susan Clark, was a very talented actress. You two were sure great in the television show *Webster*. I'm sure you miss her very much."

My question seemed to stun him a moment, and some tears started to stream down his cheeks. He fought hard to hold them back.

"My only regret was having to leave her and my kids, Tony. I miss her and them very much. I'd give anything to go back and see them again, but we're given only one go-around in life. I wish people realized just how precious life is. You should cherish every day you're alive on earth as a gift. I wish I could tell her that I loved her again. I'll see her and my kids again someday and that's what keeps me going up here."

"I've probably bothered you enough," I said.

"Absolutely not, Tony," he said. "I enjoyed meeting another Hawkeye."

"I have to ask you one more thing before you go," I said. "Did you really knock out that horse in the movie *Blazing Saddles*?"

A big grin crossed his face again.

"Heavens no, Tony," he said. "It was all trick photography. I'd never hurt an animal."

He stuck out his hand and we shook hands. He had a super strong grip. He could still play in the NFL, I thought. My hand was enveloped by his. It felt like I had just shaken hands with a bear.

"Goodbye, Tony," he said.

"Goodbye, Mr. Karras—I mean Alex," I said with a grin.

He looked at me and chuckled then started out again on his determined walk.

I watched his huge back until it disappeared into a sea of people.

"See you, Mondo," I called out.

I hoped he had heard me.

CHAPTER 12

George Washington

It was so surreal when I saw our country's first president, General George Washington, as he led a small troop of Continental Army soldiers on the road to judgment. He was dressed like a Revolutionary War General in a brilliant blue jacket with a white lapel, white pants, and gold braids on the shoulders. Shiny brass buttons glowed on his jacket, and a gold-plated sword hung from his hip. His black polished leather boots stretched almost to his knees. Silvery white long hair covered both of his ears, reminding me of his image on our U.S. one-dollar bill. He was a tall man who died in 1799 at age sixty-seven, but he looked half that age.

His men looked like they had just come from a battle. Some wore light-blue jackets and white pants that were torn and tattered and stained with blood. Others wore heavily soiled buckskin jackets and pants with crimson stains. Some still carried muskets and powder horns. I felt gratified as they approached. These were brave men who had saved our country. There was only one thing that I felt compelled to do as they neared.

I saluted.

To my surprise, General Washington ordered his troops to halt. He did a right face, stood about two feet from me, and returned my salute.

I couldn't believe it. George Washington saluted me?

He snapped his arm back to his side after his salute and stared at me. He had a rather large nose with stringy veins on the sides. If he lived today, you'd say he had rosacea.

"Stand at ease, Soldier. You must have been in the military," he said. "You gave a smart salute."

"Yes, sir, General—err, I mean Mr. President," I replied. "I was a staff sergeant in the U.S. Army in the late 1960s. I fought and was wounded in the Vietnam War. I recovered from my wounds and had a great life, sir."

A look of confusion crossed his face and his men started to murmur among themselves, wondering what had happened to the past two hundred years.

"Do you know what year it is now?" he asked.

"I think it's around 2014, the year I died, Mr. President. I passed away after minor knee surgery, and that's why I've got this green hospital gown on. But you can never tell about time up here, sir. It seemed to have stood still like there is no time. A hundred years could go by and it seems like a second, like we're in a time machine, General. You and your men have been gone many years, sir."

"That means we've been dead well over two hundred years, Soldier," he said with an amazed look on his face.

"You've been remembered in all our United States history books, Mr. President. Thank you and your men for saving our country in the Revolutionary War and the famous battle at Yorktown where you defeated the British Army. Did you know there's even a state named after you sir, the State of Washington? A huge tower called the Washington Monument was completed in 1884 and built in your honor in Washington DC.

"We owe you and your men much gratitude. The original thirteen colonies grew to fifty states, including Alaska and Hawaii. In 1996, we celebrated the two hundredth anniversary of the signing of the Declaration of Independence. And to top things off, Mr. President, your image is printed on our U.S. one-dollar bill and stamped on our quarter dollars. You're considered the father of our country, sir."

His brown eyes stared at me with another prodigious look.

"Alaska and Hawaii are now part of the United States?" he asked.

"Yes, sir. In the mid-1800s, we purchased Alaska from Russia, and it became a state along with Hawaii in 1959. It's a huge country, Mr. President."

"You said you fought in the Vietnam War, Soldier. What was that war about?" he asked.

"It was against the communists in Southeast Asia. We fought the Viet Cong and the North Vietnamese Army. There were many who felt we lost that war, Mr. President, and over fifty-eight thousand brave Americans gave up their lives. But I didn't think we lost it, sir, our country just lost the will to fight."

"Besides that war, were there many other wars after we defeated the British Army in the Revolutionary War?" he asked.

I saw that I needed to give General Washington and his men a short history lesson.

"Well, sir, unfortunately there were, and many other brave Americans died. The American Civil War between the northern and southern states over slavery was fought in the early 1860s. Our president then was Abraham Lincoln. World War I ended in 1918, and World War II in 1945. The Korean War was fought in the early 1950s, and my war, the Vietnam War, took place in the 1960s and '70s.

"The Persian Gulf War was fought in 1990, and there were wars in countries called Iraq and Afghanistan in the early 2000s. When I passed on, Mr. President, the U.S. was engaged in what's called the War on Terror against terrorists named al-Qaeda, ISIS, and the Islamic State. There are frequent terror attacks on our freedoms, sir," I said.

He shook his head with a bewildered look, and his men looked astonished and whispered among themselves. I could tell they were overwhelmed by my history briefing and the fact that they had been on the road to judgment for over two hundred years. It boggled their minds.

"Despite all the wars Mr. President, you and your men would be very proud of our country today. We have computers, cell phones, and what's called the Internet, where people can communicate with each other electronically on what we call social media, Facebook and Twitter. Oil, nuclear energy, coal, natural gas, solar and wind power helped supply us with electricity to heat and light our homes and run our factories. We have electric cars and we even placed the first man on the moon in 1969. His name was Neil Armstrong. We've had forty-four U.S. Presidents since you were first elected, sir.

"Our U.S. Armed Forces are the best in the world. We have what's known as the stealth bomber, which the enemy can't detect, and pilotless drone aircraft that can silently and deadly destroy enemy personnel and equipment from the air. Someday we could even have robot soldiers."

There was a buzz saw of excitement generated between General Washington and his troops. They couldn't believe that we had sent men into outer space. The moon, stars, and space were only something they had gazed at when they had been alive.

"We certainly could have defeated Cornwallis much earlier if we would have had all that in our time," General Washington said.

"Can I ask you a question, Mr. President?"

"You may, Soldier."

"What were men like Thomas Jefferson, John Quincy Adams, and Paul Revere really like?"

He stared at me a second, then a smile crept along his lips. I could tell that he had had some bridgework and false teeth implanted. I had read that many of his false teeth were thought to have been made of wood. But historians later wrote they were made of ivory.

"They were outstanding men and patriots, Soldier. Tom Jefferson was one of the main authors of the Declaration of Independence and my Secretary of State when I was president. John Adams was a true patriot, and Paul Revere warned us and our militia about gathering British forces," he said.

"The midnight ride of Paul Revere was made famous in all our history books, Mr. President," I said.

General Washington smiled again then turned back toward his men.

"Gentlemen, we've rested enough. We need to continue our march."

"Could I ask you one more quick question, Mr. President, before you depart?"

"Yes," he said.

"Is the story that you cut down the cherry tree really true?"

He turned around again and looked at his men, who all had smirks on their faces. They started to chuckle, and soon their chuckles turned into a roar of laughter. It felt good to have seen these men who had suffered in battle laugh and be happy. Even General Washington could hardly contain himself.

"I cannot tell a lie," he replied with a large grin. "I did cut the bark off one of my father's cherry trees when I was a youngster. Yes, it is true. Is that in the history books?"

"Yes, sir, it is," I said.

"Goodbye, Soldier," he said. "We have to move on. You didn't tell me your name."

"I'm Tony Powers from West Des Moines, Iowa, Mr. President. Iowa became a state in 1846 and it lies right in the middle of the country between the Missouri and Mississippi Rivers."

"Thank you for the excellent briefing," he said. "Good luck in eternity."

I saluted the famous general and his men one more time.

They all returned my salute, then picked up their gear, regrouped, and started their march on the road to judgment again.

I stood in awe as I watched the father of our country and his men march away into a throng of humanity and then disappear from my view.

They were such wonderful and brave men, I thought. I knew our Creator would give them a fair shake someday.

I was never more proud to have been an American.

CHAPTER 13

Al Couppee

We all have had a special person or mentor who had a special influence in our lives and careers. Mine was former University of Iowa Ironman quarterback Al Couppee. When I spotted him on the road to judgment, my mind raced back in time about forty years when he had first hired me.

Al had passed away in 1998 at the age of seventy-eight. He approached in a tan suit and walked with a quick stride. He looked years younger but still had that famous snow-white hair. He always kind of reminded me of Santa Claus without the beard and famous red suit. He was an Iowa Hawkeye forever. The black-and-gold tie he wore attested to that.

"Hi, Coup," I called out. "Remember me?"

His brisk walk slowed down, and he stared at me with large blue eyes behind a pair of brown glasses.

"I'll be darned," he said with a shocked look. "How in the name of Jesus, Mary, and Joseph did you get up here?"

"It was pretty easy, Al," I replied. "I passed away after minor knee surgery. My heart stopped, and they couldn't get it started again. The Good Lord decided to call me right off the operating table." I laughed softly.

He stuck out a big meaty hand for me to shake.

"It's great to see you again, Tony. How many years has it been?"

"It's been a bunch, Al. You look great. God's been good to you," I said.

"Don't speak too soon. I haven't been judged yet," he said with a smile.

"I always wanted to thank you personally for hiring me as a producer way back in 1972 at KGTV in San Diego. That was my first television job. I couldn't believe it when I walked into the newsroom to drop off my resume and there you sat in the sports office. I remembered the nameplate on your desk. It read 'Al Couppee, Sports Director.' I said to myself, *Hey, he's famous back in Iowa.*"

"You should also remember that I tried to talk you out of a radio and television career. There was way too much backbiting and backstabbing in the business in those days. But I guess you decided to tough it out anyway," he said.

"I remember my first audition behind the anchor desk. You ran out of the director's booth and said I was terrible. I was very nervous then and I flubbed a lot of words."

"Honestly, you were awful back then. I never thought you'd be as successful as you were in the broadcasting business," he said.

"Al, you also helped me land the job as a sports anchor reporter at WHO-TV in Des Moines. I never forgot that too. You had a big influence with Jim Zabel and the folks back in Iowa. You were known as Mr. Sports in San Diego in the 1970s, Coup. I remember when you sent me out to do my first big interview. It was with Arnold Palmer. I'll never forget the night we covered the Major League Baseball's Old-Timers Game. Casey Stengel, Mickey Mantle, and Yogi Berra were all there. You were the master of ceremonies, and there were thirty thousand people in the stands. They loved you in San Diego, Coup."

"It was a great job, Tony, but unfortunately the consultants took over the television news business and they thought I was too old and too corny to do television sports anymore. It happened to a lot of folks in the business," he said.

"The same thing happened to me, Al, in the twilight of my sports television career. But boy have I got a surprise for you."

His big blue eyes got even bigger behind his glasses.

"What kind of surprise?" he asked.

"I met Nile Kinnick up here. We even played a little catch. He spoke very highly of you."

A look of complete disbelief spread over his face. His normally red patchy cheeks turned ashen. He looked like he was ready to faint. Then lines of tears started to flow down his face, and he wept for a couple of minutes before he regained his composure.

"You saw Nile," he said as he wiped his eyes with his fingers. "I'd give anything to have seen him again. He was one of the greatest persons I ever knew. I'm convinced he would have become President of the United States had he lived. How in God's heaven could you have seen him, Tony, with all this humanity from around the world marching on the road to judgment? It'd be like spotting a needle in a haystack."

"I believed it was shortly after I arrived up here, Al," I said. "He just seemed to appear out of nowhere, but the black-and-gold sweater with the big gold 'I' on the front caught my attention and made him stand out to me. Once I said I was from Iowa, that got his attention too. You're right, Al. What a great person he was. He loved to talk about the 1939 Iowa Ironmen and you. He wanted to know about Iowa City, and I told him they named Kinnick Stadium after him. That really pleased him."

"Do you think he's very far ahead of us on the road to judgment?" he asked.

"Boy, Al, I couldn't tell you if I saw him yesterday, three months ago, or last year. Time doesn't seem to move up here. It's like time stood still. Remember Rod Serling in the *Twilight Zone?* That's how it feels up here. He'd say you've traveled through another dimension, a dimension of not only sight and sound but of mind. A journey into a wondrous land whose boundaries are that of imagination. That's the signpost dead ahead, your next stop, the Twilight Zone. I'm convinced, Al, that we're kind of in that dimension he talked about.

"But I'm also convinced if you really wanted to find someone up here, all you'd have to do is think about them and start looking. I've already met a number of Iowa and famous national icons here. I was really thrilled when I met JFK and George Washington and some of his troops."

He stared at me with another look of incredulousness.

"You mean to tell me you actually spoke to JFK and George Washington?"

"They were as far from me as you are now, Al, two feet away. It was incredible. I told JFK I was sorry that he had been assassinated and I shouldn't have even mentioned it. I was like someone in the press corps who asked a dumb question. It ended our conversation, and he just walked away. If I see him again I'm going to apologize to him."

"I cried when he died," Al said. "But how could you have seen George Washington? He lived in the seventeenth century, for heaven's sake."

"It doesn't seem to make any difference up here, Al. We're all in the present here. There doesn't seem to be any past either. I was never prouder to have been an American after I had spoken to him and his men. They were such brave patriots. I brought them up to date on historical events, and they couldn't believe we placed a man on the moon."

I reached into the pocket of my hospital gown and showed Al the three jelly beans President Reagan had given me.

"Will you look at these?" I said. "All I did was mention WHO Radio, and President Reagan and his huge dog Lucky stopped by for a chat on their way to judgment. He looked great and he loved WHO and his jelly beans."

Al was flabbergasted.

"Ron was one of my best friends in life, Tony. He loved Nile and the Ironmen too. When I did television sports, he was governor of California. We'd call each other about once a week and talk about the old days in Iowa. I loved the man," he said as several new tears flowed down his cheeks.

"They're all up here. Hopefully you'll see them on the way to judgment. I really hope you'll see Nile again," I said. "What did you miss most about your life, Al?" I asked.

He thought for a second, then scratched some of the white hair on top of his head.

"I wish I could go back and relive it, Tony. First and foremost, I miss my family. I wish I could tell them how much I love them again. I loved announcing Iowa football on KRNT Radio in Des Moines before I went to San Diego. I loved broadcasting the San Diego Chargers games on KOGO Radio. I loved playing quarterback for the 1939 Iowa Ironmen and handing the ball off to Nile Kinnick and watching him make all those incredible runs. I loved serving in the United States Navy and driving my big Cadillacs.

"I loved attending the Friday Night boxing matches in San Diego and serving on the California Boxing Commission. I loved doing all those things, Tony, but I also look forward to judgment day when I will face the Good Lord. I felt I made a difference with my life. Sure, there were certain people and athletes that I had grudges with but I've forgiven them all. I have no ill will toward anyone. I can't complain, Tony. I had a great life and I'm looking forward to eternity, especially if I can meet Nile and the Ironmen again, but I won't get there if I keep talking to you."

"If that's a hint that you want to leave, Al, you have my blessing," I said with a chuckle. "Besides, I've got some other folks I'd love to run into again, like old JZ."

He let out a hearty "ho ho ho" laugh, just like Santa Claus.

"If you see him, Tony, tell him I always thought he was the biggest cheapskate I ever knew. I'm just kidding, Lord."

"JZ always told me this story about you doing play-by-play of an Iowa football game once on KRNT Radio. Bob Jeter had broken loose on a long run and you called it like this: 'He's at the twenty—he's at the thirty—he's at the forty—he's at the fifty—look at that son of a buck run, folks!' But you didn't exactly say buck but that other B-word," I said with a chuckle.

Al put one of his big fingers up to his lips.

"Shhhhh," he said. "I don't want God to hear that, Tony. I confess I did get a little excited and accidentally said that. That darn Zabel didn't let anything get by him. I hope the Good Lord forgave me."

"I'm sure he already has," I said.

We shook hands, and he gave me a huge bear hug.

"I'm proud of you, Tony. You made it in broadcasting when I thought you wouldn't. Goodbye."

"Goodbye, Al. I hope you see Nile."

"I hope so too," he said. "But it's the Lord's call."

I watched him as he made his way back into the never-ending line of people and pets on the road to judgment. His white hair stood out in a sea of dark hair, and then he melted away into the throng.

"Please, heavenly Father," I prayed, "let him reunite with his old pal Nile someday."

CHAPTER 14

Jim Valvano

I was a huge fan of the hit television series *Fantasy Island* in the 1980s. The show opened with actor Herve Villechaize, who yelled, "The plane! The plane!" and Ricardo Montalban, who was dressed in a dazzling all-white suit. I thought of the show when I noticed iconic college basketball coach "Jimmy V" Jim Valvano walking on the road to judgment. He too was dressed in a brilliant white suit but with a red tie. He wore matching red socks and brilliant white dress shoes. He almost looked like a guardian angel without wings. He'll be forever remembered for the classic line in his ESPN ESPYS speech, "Don't give up, don't ever give up," in his valiant fight against cancer.

He passed away in 1993 at age forty-seven.

I had the chance to interview him in the late 1980s at WHO-TV. He was speaking at a benefit at Drake University. I remember how gracious and funny he was back then when I approached him for the interview. Amazingly, he looked the same on the road to judgment. He had the same black hair combed straight back on his head and a wide smile that revealed a small gap in his front teeth. He had coached North Carolina State to the 1983 college basketball national championship, and the sports shows still air the video today of him running around the court after the fifty-four to fifty-two victory over Houston.

"Hey, Coach V," I called out. "You look like you just came from Fantasy Island."

He stopped and stared at me with a startled look for a moment, then laughed.

"And you look like you just came from the hospital," he said with his raspy New Jersey accent. "That was one of my favorite television shows too, especially Ricardo Montalban dressed in that white suit. But as you can see, I had to add a little red to include the NC State colors. How did you end up here, my friend?"

"I went in for minor knee surgery and it somehow turned fatal, coach," I said. "I never made it out of the operating room."

He strolled up to me and shook my hand with a firm grip.

"I'm sorry to hear that. Did you sue them?" he asked with an amused look. "With whom do I have the great pleasure of speaking to?"

"I'm Tony Powers from West Des Moines, Iowa, coach, and no, I didn't sue them personally because that would have been a little hard to do up here," I said smiling. "I worked at WHO-TV in Des Moines and interviewed you in the late 1980s for our television sports segment. You were in town for a speaking engagement. We talked about your unbelievable 1983 title and, of course, your famous run around the court after the game. You looked like a chicken with its head cut off. Did you finally find someone to hug, Coach V?"

"I was so happy I hugged air," he said with a boisterous New Jersey type laugh. "I would have hugged the janitor if he had been there. I would have hugged anyone, even you in the hospital clothes."

"Hey, coach, you look like a guardian angel in your white suit," I said.

"Well, I'd sure love to be," he said with a chuckle. "But I've been on the road to judgment since my death. Maybe I'll score a few points at my judgment with this suit. Let's hope the Good Lord is a North Carolina State fan."

"If he judged us based on our clothing, I'd be in real trouble, coach," I said.

He looked me up and down and then burst out laughing.

"You might have a point there, Tony, but I'm just kidding," he said. "There are not too many places to hide up here. Besides, he's going to look deep into your soul, not your clothes."

"Coach V, everybody remembered your famous cancer speech at the ESPYS and what an inspirational speech it was," I said. "Your V Foundation has raised millions of dollars for cancer research and the hope to someday find a cure for cancer. God's going to smile when he judges you, sir. You did a great deal for mankind besides win basketball games."

His ever-present smiling face turned solemn and his big eyes turned moist.

"I certainly didn't want my life to end, Tony. I had a beautiful wife and three daughters and forty-seven good years on earth. We can beat cancer someday, but we've got to have the will to beat it too. That's why we have to fight on and not be discouraged because the chemo treatments will sap your strength and test your resolve. That's why I said don't give up, don't ever give up at the ESPY's. Because if you do, then you're done and cancer has won. We can never let it beat us, Tony.

"I told folks before I passed on to live their lives to the fullest and to make sure that you laugh and cry every day. As a coach, I was inspired by Green Bay Packers coach Vince Lombardi and by that sensational tennis player Arthur Ashe. I only hope that my life served as a role model for our future athletes and coaches. I'll say it again: don't give up, don't ever give up in everything you do."

"You certainly inspired me, coach. Maybe the Good Lord will reward you with that guardian angel position," I said.

A big smile returned to his face.

"If he does, I hope he'll assign me to my friend Dick Vitale. He needs all the help he can get," he said with a chuckle.

"I interviewed Dick and his broadcast partner Mike Patrick at an Iowa-Purdue basketball game once, coach," I said. "I asked Patrick what it was like to work with Vitale. He said it was like the mental patients taking over the asylum."

Coach V laughed and laughed at my comment. It felt so good to see this famous coach enjoy himself. He then stuck out his hand as his signal that he was ready to continue his march on the road to judgment. He slapped his hand against mine.

"Tony, it was great to meet you again. I hope I made a difference in your life as well," he said.

"You bet, Coach V. I'm going to search for a white suit just like yours."

"Maybe St. Peter could help you find one," he said with a giant smirk. "Goodbye, Tony."

"Goodbye, Coach V," I said.

I watched as he continued his journey on the road to judgment. There was no doubt in my mind that he would make it to heaven. He went out a winner. The back of his white suit seemed to glow as he made his way through the throng of humanity and animals. Then he was gone.

His words "don't give up, don't ever give up," echoed in my ears.

CHAPTER 15

Harry Caray

One of the highlights of my eighteen-year sports broadcasting career was meeting and doing an interview with Chicago Cubs and Baseball Hall of Fame announcer Harry Caray at Wrigley Field in Chicago in the early 1980s. So I couldn't believe it when I spotted Harry in the throngs of people walking toward judgment day. He stood out like a sore thumb, if you could excuse the expression. Most noticeable were the huge black-rimmed eyeglasses he wore along with his snow-white hair and dark-blue Chicago Cubs jacket with the big white letters CUBS on the front.

He had passed away in 1988 at the age of eighty-three. He never got to see his beloved Cubs win the World Series after they beat the Cleveland Indians in 2016. Their first World Series victory in 108 years. His announcing always included his hallmark phrase, "Holy cow!" when describing an exciting play or home run. So to get his attention, I called out those legendary words when he passed by.

"Holy cow!" I cried out as he lumbered past me.

He wheeled around to face me, and I couldn't believe how magnificent he appeared. He didn't look a day over sixty, and those big eyes and glasses of his perused me.

"You must be a Cubs fan," he said, laughing.

"Hi, Harry," I said, extending my hand for him to shake. "I'm Tony Powers. Actually, I'm a New York Yankees fan. I interviewed you in the early 1980s at Wrigley Field when I was a sportscaster at

WHO-TV in Des Moines, Iowa. I was doing a story on the Iowa Cubs, who had made it to the majors. You were a great interview. That's when you worked with Steve Stone as your color man at WGN-TV."

"Glad to meet you again, Tony," he said as he eyed my green hospital garb. "You should be wearing your Yankees colors," he quipped. "You've got a great memory. What happened to you, Tony? Did you pass away in the hospital?"

"I think so, Harry. I went in for meniscus knee surgery, and once they anesthezied me, I was gone."

"What year was that?" he asked.

"In 2014, Harry."

"Holy cow!" he exclaimed. "You mean I've been dead all this time and I still have not made it to judgment day."

"If God is a Cubs fan, Harry, you'll be rewarded forever," I said with a laugh. "What did you miss the most about your life, Harry?"

"Oh, Tony," he said as his eyes glazed over a bit. "I miss my family and friends so much. If only I could broadcast one more game at Wrigley Field and sing 'Take Me Out to the Ballgame' during the seventh-inning stretch. I would have loved to see the Cubs win a World Series, Tony. I would love to be able to drink another Budweiser beer, but don't tell the Good Lord that. I would love to see Sammy Sosa hit another home run and Ferguson Jenkins pitch another no-hitter.

"I'd love to see Ernie Banks, Ron Santo, Billy Williams, Mark Grace, Rick Sutcliffe, Ryne Sandburg, and all the famous Cubs again. I'd love to walk around Wrigley Field one more time and go out and touch the ivy-covered outfield wall. I would love to announce 'Cubs win! Cubs win!' one more time, Tony. We're giving only one go-around, and I had a great life, no complaints."

He took a white handkerchief out of the pocket of his Cubs jacket, removed his big dark-rimmed glasses, and dabbed away the tears that had formed around his eyes. He blew his nose. I could see the fornlornness in his face. I decided to talk a little baseball again.

"What did you think of your top farm team, the Iowa Cubs, Harry? Many of the Chicago Cubs played some of their minor league careers in Des Moines."

"I loved Des Moines, Tony, and my good friend Jim Zabel at WHO Radio and TV. You're right, Des Moines supplied us with many key players over the years," he said, putting his huge eyeglasses back on. "You said you thought you passed away in the hospital, Tony. What did you mean by that? Are you saying you don't know whether you're dead or not?" he asked.

"Are you really dead, Tony?" Harry Asked. "Well, I don't know, Harry. When I played some golf with Coach Johnny Orr up here, they wouldn't give me any golf knickers to wear. They told Johnny I wasn't qualified to wear them yet. So yes, maybe I'm not quite deceased yet."

"Holy cow!" Harry bellowed and snapped his head back with a hearty laugh. "Are they giving you some kind of tour first?" he said with a chuckle.

"As strange as it sounds, Harry, I believe so. I don't feel dead. I threw the football with Nile Kinnick, played golf with Coach Orr, shot arrows with Olympic gold medalist archer Doreen Wilber, saluted our first president George Washington, and received some jelly beans from former president and former WHO Radio sports-caster Ronald Reagan. And I just talked Cubs baseball with you, Harry. How could I be dead?"

Harry looked absolutely perplexed at my comments.

"Well, I know I'm dead, Tony," he declared. "If I wasn't, I'd still be broadcasting Cubs games at Wrigley Field instead of walking this long road to judgment day. I'd better get back in line, Tony. It was a real pleasure to have talked some Cubs baseball with you." He extended his right hand for me to shake.

"Harry, I couldn't have been more honored, sir," I said quickly accepting his hand. "I hope you get to see the Good Lord soon and he sends you right to heaven—Cubs heaven."

He turned and stepped back into the line of folks who were headed to final judgment. I could see the big red letter C with a white trim on the back of his blue Cubs jacket as he slowly disappeared from my view. I actually thought I could hear him sing in a raspy and deep voice, "Take me out to the ballgame. Take me out to the crowd. Buy me some peanuts and crackerjacks. I don't care if I never get back. So it's root, root, root for the Cubbies..."

CHAPTER 16

Christopher Columbus

When I spotted Christopher Columbus on the road to judgment, I had to pinch myself twice to believe it. I was more shocked than when I had met Nile Kinnick or George Washington earlier. This was the man whom historians proclaimed to have discovered America. We even celebrate Columbus Day every October. He had a magnificent appearance as he approached, the same look that had been illustrated in my grade-school history books.

He wore a flowing, bright red robe with a huge white cross emblazoned on the front. A large black hat adorned his head with a large brown feather stuck in it. I noticed a gold chest protector under the robe like the kind that Spanish conquistadors often wore. He was a stout man about six feet tall and had long blond hair on the sides but thin hair on top. He had a short beard and mustache. He looked very much the part of a legendary world explorer. He had passed away in 1506 at age fifty-four.

I knew he spoke Spanish and Italian but wondered if he knew English. I should ask him as he walked by, I thought.

"Buenos dias, Señor Columbus. Hables ingles?" I asked.

He stopped walking, turned, and stared at me with large, penetrating blue eyes. Then he smiled and showed very good-looking white teeth.

"Si," he said.

"You're Christopher Columbus and you discovered America," I said.

His white teeth flashed again and he laughed.

"Some have said I discovered America and others have said I didn't," he said. "What do you think, my friend?"

"I believed my sixth grade history book," I said with a smile. "It said you discovered America in 1492 with your ship, the *Santa Maria*. We even celebrate Columbus Day every October."

"Then I discovered America," he said with a laugh. "I know we came on shore in the Bahamas during our first voyage. There were all these little islands, and then we even visited the southern tip of what you call Florida today. We encountered the Seminole Indians there. They didn't quite know what to think of us with our silver helmets and shields. We had guns, and they didn't. They were very afraid of us. There were also plenty of huge cypress trees and sawgrass as far as the eye could see. I believe you would call that the Everglades today. There were swamps, snakes, and all these black alligators. The beaches were very nice, though, just like the ones we had in Spain."

"You also discovered Puerto Rico in 1493," I said. "It might become the United States's fifty-first state someday."

"Oh yes, the Caribbean and its striking blue waters. Very nice," he said.

He studied me and my hospital clothes for another long moment.

"What happened to you, my friend, and when did you die?" he asked.

"I passed away after minor knee surgery in 2014. These are the clothes they gave me in the hospital. I guess I went so quick, there wasn't time for a change of clothes," I said with a chuckle.

"I'm so sorry you died so young. We didn't have much surgery in my day except for some leeches the physicians would place on you to bleed you. I died at an early age myself," he said.

"I had a good life, though, as a radio and television sports announcer," I said. "Oh sure, there were some things I should have done in life and other things I did that I regretted. I'll have to answer to God for those someday. I see where you passed in 1506. That was five hundred years ago, sir, and you still look great."

He shook his head with amazement.

"I've been on the road to judgment for a long time, then," he said with a pensive look. "To me, it felt like I passed on only yesterday. I think I lived a good life also. I don't think the Good Lord will judge me on whether I discovered America or not. It's how I lived my life that will count in the end. I know I had an impact on the lives of a lot of people. I think I helped spread the Word of God to the New World, just like the apostles did two thousand years ago.

"We encountered some hostiles whom we were forced to kill or enslave. I regretted having to do that and hope God forgives me for any transgressions against the peoples of the New World. But to some, we were invaders. They wanted to fight us. Maybe the Lord has punished me by making me wander these hundreds of years."

"He's made us all walk on the road to judgment," I said. "Time has no meaning up here, whether it's a day, a week, a year, or a thousand years. We're in eternity forever. He'll treat you fairly, Mr. Columbus. I'm sure of that."

"Call me Christopher," he said.

"You can call me Tony," I said.

"Ah, Tony, what a great name," he said with a laugh.

"The history books said you actually made four different trips to the New World," I said.

"Si. I was commissioned four times and discovered new lands each trip. We had to rely on ocean currents and the trade winds in those days. We founded islands in the Caribbean and even landed in Cuba and discovered Central America. The voyages were very trying as we had to fight diseases and storms along the way."

"What do you think was your biggest accomplishment in life?" I asked.

He pondered my question for a moment, then stared at our beautiful planet Earth situated far below us. His blue eyes turned reflective and misted over.

"That I made some contribution for the betterment of our planet, Tony," he said. "Just look at our wonderful world down there.

I discovered parts of it and helped put those places on the map for future generations and explorers. I also helped spread the Word of God, and I hope the Good Lord will give me some credit for that on my judgment day. I miss my family terribly and I hope I'll be reunited with them someday in eternity. You said they celebrate Columbus Day every October, Tony. I don't want any praise, just forgiveness."

I stood in awe as I listened to this great world icon and explorer. I was amazed at how humble he was. Having discovered America was no small feat, but this man wanted only forgiveness for his sins and not any exultations. I was impressed and I knew he wanted to continue his march on the road to judgment. I stuck out my hand and shook his with a firm grip.

"I wanted to tell you how thrilled I am to have met you, Christopher. You're a world icon and a real credit to all of mankind. Our world will never forget you," I said.

A large smile returned to his face, and his white teeth glistened again. He placed both hands on my shoulders.

"The pleasure was all mine, Tony. What was your last name?" he asked.

"Powers. Anthony—err, I mean Tony Powers," I said with a chuckle.

"I'll remember you always, Anthony Powers," he said also with a bright smile.

I watched him as he resumed his place among the thousands and millions of souls on the road to judgment. He soon disappeared into the great mass of humanity that moved like a giant wagon train from the Old West. Person after person in a constant stream of motion. *Can you imagine it?* I thought. Christopher Columbus said he would remember me.

I got goose bumps just thinking about it.

CHAPTER 17

Tait and Jim Cummins

I'd never had the chance to meet the legendary eastern Iowa broadcaster and sportswriter Tait Cummins in real life. I had heard a lot of stories about him from Jim Zabel. But I had been good friends with Tait's nephew, veteran NBC News reporter Jim Cummins. That's why I was so surprised to have seen them walking together on the road to judgment. Both had been excellent news journalists their entire lives.

Jim passed away in 2007 at age sixty-two. Tait passed away in 1984 at age seventy-eight. Tait was dressed in a black pinstriped suit with a white shirt and a black-and-gold striped tie. He had thin black hair that covered the back portion of his head, and he walked proudly with a big smile. He had a look like he really enjoyed himself, smiling and bantering as he walked.

Jim wore a tan suit with a white shirt and large pink tie. He had a full head of black hair tinged with a little gray. I'd always thought he looked like a cross between former NBC News anchor Tom Brokaw and former Fox News anchor Brit Hume. Tom was a big Iowa Hawkeye fan, and Jim was too. He too walked with a chuckle like Tait had just told him a joke or something.

I waved my right arm and got their attention.

"Hey, Jim Cummins, NBC News, remember me?" I yelled.

Jim walked up to me, and I could see in his face that he searched for an answer.

"I think I know you," he said as he extended his hand for me to shake.

"Tony Powers, WHO-TV in Des Moines, Jim," I said. "You used to come back and visit the sports department every time you covered a story in Des Moines. You loved to talk about Iowa football and your dear uncle Tait."

"Toooony," he said as a look of recognition crossed his features. "Yes, I remember you, my friend. Let me introduce you to my uncle Tait."

Tait beamed as I shook his hand.

"I'd heard a lot about you, Tait, from my old boss Jim Zabel," I said.

"I hope you didn't believe any of those stories about me from Z," he said with a chuckle.

"You're both certainly Iowa icons," I said. "Jim, you were a star basketball player at Cedar Rapids Regis and Northwestern, then had a brilliant news broadcasting career with NBC. Tait, Iowans remembered you as the voice of WMT Radio Sports and your classic play-by-play of Cedar Rapids high school sports and Iowa football and basketball. Before that, you were a fabulous sportswriter for the *Cedar Rapids Gazette* and even won a Pulitzer Prize. You guys did it all."

"Tony, thank you for all those kind tributes," Jim said. "But Uncle Tait and I still have to appear before God and face our judgments, just like you. We both had fine and happy lives and hoped you had one too."

"You're right, Jim. We can talk all we want about what we accomplished on earth, but up here it's a different story. I think sometimes we get carried away with our honors and awards, but they don't mean a hill of beans up here. We're born into this world with nothing and we left it with nothing. Nevertheless, you two will be remembered for many years on what you did on the planet. I'm sure the Good Lord will take that all into consideration in his final judgment."

"What happened to you, Tony?" Tait said as he eyed my hospital garb. "Did you have some sort of accident or illness?"

"Would you believe, Tait, that I died after minor meniscus surgery on my left knee?" I said with a laugh. "Something happened after they put me under. I went to sleep, started to dream, and just never woke up. I wish they had a mall up here where I could go buy a nice suit."

We all laughed.

"Jim, what do you remember most about your famous uncle Tait?" I asked.

He stared at him a moment with a proud look in his eyes.

"He was the best uncle you could ask for, Tony. I looked up to him all of my life," he said. "You're right when you called him an Iowa icon because that's what he was. He did a lot for less fortunate people and helped raise a ton of money for charities. The city of Cedar Rapids named an entire sports complex after him because they were so proud of him. He actually knew the great Nile Kinnick and all of the Iowa Ironmen."

Tait put his arm around his nephew and hugged him. He had tears in his eyes.

"I was never a prouder uncle," he said. "Jim was an outstanding network news reporter and was the bureau chief for NBC News in Dallas, Tony. That's how much they respected him in the television news business. And he wasn't a bad college basketball player at Northwestern either."

"You were known for your very descriptive and humorous play-by-play on WMT Radio in Cedar Rapids, Tait," I said.

A big grin emerged on Tait's face.

"I loved to have fun broadcasting the games, Tony, and not only on the field. I looked for interesting things to talk about around the stadiums. I remembered one Iowa Hawkeye football game. I noticed a young couple sitting in the stands. She kissed him on first down, he kissed her on second down, then she kissed him on third down, and he kissed her back on fourth down, and I broadcasted it all on the air," he said, laughing.

"Jim, whenever there was a big news story in Iowa, you were there to cover it for NBC News, like the Great Flood of 1993 or the Iowa Caucuses," I said.

A pleasant, reflective smile appeared on his face.

"I loved covering big stories in Iowa, Tony," he said. "It was like my second home. I loved visiting WHO-TV every time I was in Des Moines and seeing you in the sports department. We talked about everything from the Hawkeyes to Nile Kinnick to Uncle Tait to the Chicago Cubs. You were a fine sports reporter and a good friend."

"Thank you, Jim. I really appreciate that. Speaking of Nile Kinnick, I thought you guys would like to know I had the chance to meet him up here," I said.

A shocked look crossed both of their faces.

"You saw the great Nile Kinnick up here?" Tait said.

"Yes, sir. We even played catch and ran a few short pass patterns. He's one of the first people I met when I ventured into eternity. He was really a nice guy. He couldn't believe the University of Iowa named their football stadium after him. It made my day—I mean my eternity to meet him, I'll tell you. You could tell he was a phenomenal human being who had touched so many," I said. "I also met JFK and President Reagan up here."

Jim's shocked expression turned into one of incredulity.

"You met two of our greatest presidents up here, Tony?" he asked.

I reached into the pocket of my hospital shirt and pulled out the red, white, and blue jelly beans and showed it to them.

"That's right, Jim. President Reagan and I reminisced about WHO Radio, and he gave me these souvenirs. I'll never eat them," I said. "I'll cherish them for all eternity."

"Wow, we're talking to a real celebrity here, Uncle Tait," Jim said. "Ronald Reagan loved jelly beans."

"I'm certainly no celebrity," I said. "When I reach final judgment, it will be just me and the Good Lord. There's no celebrity up here. For some reason, I think God allowed me to recognize and meet some famous people up here. Every one of them was very humble despite their greatness on earth. We all left our world with nothing, but I'll always have these jelly beans to remember it by. I kind of wish I was dressed in a nice suit before I meet God," I said with an exasperated look. "You two certainly look great. He should be very impressed with both of you."

"I'm sure he'll be pleased with you, Tony, despite your wardrobe," Jim said with a grin.

"You'd better have underwear on, mister," Tait said behind a roar of laughter.

When we finished our laugh, we shook hands and exchanged hugs. In eternity, we were all like family. We all faced the same judgment, whether we were award-winning journalists, presidents, Olympic gold medalists, star football players, actors, comedians, or championship coaches. One other thing I discovered about Jim was that both of our wives' first names were Connie. We had a bond even in eternity.

I watched as they disappeared back into the throng on the road to judgment. It was like a giant, never-ending road that stretched as far as the eye could see into the distance before extending into a great white cloud. A giant sea of people moved ever so slowly into the cloud. God had to be in that cloud, I thought. Was he sitting on some giant throne, I wondered, surrounded by all his angels and saints? Would his judgment be quick and final? Would we have a chance to explain our lives and plead our case, so to speak? What would he look like? I hoped that I wouldn't have to walk hundreds of years before being judged.

I thought once again of Tait and Jim and I felt happy as well as sad for having known and laughed with them. I would miss them.

I started my long walk again.

Who would I meet next?

CHAPTER 18

Bob Feller

I had been a huge fan of Bob Feller ever since my Little League days pitching for the Altoona, Iowa, Yanks. So I was pleasantly surprised when I recognized the former Cleveland Indians fireballer on the road to judgment. After eighteen major league seasons and three no-hitters, the Major League Baseball Hall of Famer had passed away in 2010 at age ninety-two. He looked half that age as he walked triumphantly toward judgment day.

He wore a white shirt with khaki pants and a navy-blue tie. What distinguished him from the crowd was his fire-engine-red baseball cap on his head with the image of Chief Wahoo emblazoned on the front, the logo of the Cleveland Indians. He looked happy, like he had just pitched another no-hitter. I remembered when I had faced his fastball back in 1985 in a media game before an Iowa Cubs contest at the old Sec Taylor Stadium in Des Moines.

I had dug my tennis shoes into the dirt at home plate as I awaited his first pitch. He was in his late sixties at the time, but the ball buzzed by my ear like an angry bee. I made a feeble swing. Strike one. His next pitch was a slow, looping curveball. I swung and hit nothing but air again. Strike two. I got very frustrated.

"C'mon, Bob, give me something good to hit," I had yelled. "You're making me look bad."

He stared at me from the mound and a big smile crossed his face. He made a big windup and delivered a perfect batting practice pitch, waist high and right down the middle.

I took a deep breath and swung as hard as I could.

Craaaaack was the sound that echoed throughout the stadium as the ball traveled to right center field and dropped to the ground for a single. The crowd cheered, and I felt like I was on cloud nine as I ran toward first base.

He had looked over at me from the mound and winked.

Back on the road to judgment, I watched as he started to walk by me, completely unaware of my presence.

"You're the famous Heater from Van Meter," I said to get his attention. "I got a base hit off you once."

He slowed his walk, stopped, and stared at me with a surprised look.

"I hope not," he said with a chuckle. "I hope you weren't wearing that outfit when you did."

"Don't worry, Bob, I wasn't," I said. "I'm Tony Powers from West Des Moines, Iowa. I worked as a sportscaster at WHO-TV in Des Moines, and you grooved me a pitch once at the old Sec Taylor Stadium, now called beautiful Principal Park. You also struck out Jim Zabel that day."

"Why are you all decked out in that hospital shirt, Tony?" he said.

"Knee surgery gone bad," I said. "I didn't wake up after they put me under."

"That's too bad," he said as he shook my hand with a baseball pitcher's strong grip. "I'm sorry to hear that, but glad you at least got a hit off me."

"You're an Iowa icon, Bob from Van Meter. You'll be remembered forever as the Cleveland Indians fastballer and Hall of Famer. It's too bad your museum in Van Meter had to close. But after you passed away, they had a very hard time keeping it open. I visited there before I passed and saw a baseball that you had signed. It read, 'I struck out Joe DiMaggio,' and it had your signature on the ball. I wish now I had bought it. They wanted two hundred dollars for it."

"Well, Tony, I'm glad you didn't buy it. It wouldn't have done you any good up here," he said with a smile. "I feel bad they had to close my museum, though."

"They shipped everything to Cleveland," I said. "Even a bat signed by the immortal Babe Ruth. I remember driving by the farmhouse that you grew up in in Van Meter. A doctor lives there now with his kids."

A nostalgic look appeared on his face and his eyes turned serious.

"I had a great life, Tony. I grew up on an Iowa farm and got to pitch in the major leagues. I miss my family and my sons and would give anything to be able to go back. But we're only given one go-around and that's why we should cherish every second of our lives on earth. The Good Lord won't care whether I struck out Joe DiMaggio or whether I'm in Cooperstown or an Iowa icon. He'll ask me what I did for my fellow man and whether I kept his commandments. But I'm ready to face him. What about you, Tony?"

"That's well put, Bob," I said. "I had a great life cut short by an accident in the hospital. That's why Jesus always told us that we'll never know the day or the hour that we're called into eternity. If I were ever given a second chance at life, I'd live it to the fullest each and every day. I'd jump out of bed every morning and shout for joy, happy that I was alive. But I do look forward to facing the heavenly Father just like all these other folks on the road to judgment. I know he'll treat each and every one of us fairly. But it wouldn't be right, Bob, if I didn't ask you a couple of baseball questions like a good sports reporter would."

"Fire away," he said.

"The media once reported that your fastest pitch ever was clocked around one hundred five miles per hour. Was that accurate?"

"I'd say that's pretty close, give or take a mile," he said with a grin.

"They said you once pitched against a speeding motorcycle going one hundred miles per hour and your fastball beat it to the finish line?"

He laughed out loud at my question.

"Yes, that was a true story. I think it was a Harley. I don't know who thought that one up, but it sure made a great story in the newspapers," he said fondly.

"Who were the toughest hitters you ever faced?" I asked.

"Oh, definitely Joe DiMaggio and Ted Williams. You were lucky to get anything by them, even my best fastball. But I got them out swinging a few times, and they didn't like it," he said.

"Should Pete Rose ever be elected into the Hall of Fame?"

"He was one of the greatest players ever, Tony, but who am I to judge? When Pete arrives up here, he'll be judged on how he lived his life and not on how he played baseball. I'll be judged on my life and not on my fastball. You'll be judged on how you lived your life, Tony, and not whether you were a good sports reporter. Judge not lest ye be judged, sayeth the Lord. I hope he gets in someday," he said.

"You had over twenty-five hundred strikeouts in your career, but you also gave up a lot of walks. How did you explain that?" I asked.

He ran his hand over his chin and pondered my question for a moment. Then he smiled.

"I was blessed with a tremendous arm, Tony. Many hitters couldn't get their bat around on many of my pitches so they went to the plate, sat on pitches, and hoped to draw a walk. Many times they got the benefit of the umpire's call to get themselves on base. But when you threw as hard as I did, sometimes my fastball would sail a little when it hit the plate and out of the strike zone," he said.

"What were some of your greatest moments in life?" I asked.

He became a little glassy-eyed, and I could see that my question greatly affected him.

"I remembered playing catch with my dad as a youngster on the farm, Tony. You remember the hit move *Field of Dreams* when Kevin Costner played catch with his father? I played catch with my dad and got to know him really well. It meant a lot to me. He helped me develop my curveball at a young age on the farm. I'll never forget my years in the Navy in World War II and when we won the 1948 World Series and my three no-hitters. Or when I was inducted into the Hall of Fame in 1962, and when the Indians retired my number 19.

"I'll always remember my family and the birth of my sons and growing up on the farm. If only I could go back one more time and walk around the pasture and fields again and play catch with my dad once more. I'll never forget my dad and mom. I'll love them forever," he said as the tears slowly rolled down his face.

I knew then that it was time to let him get back on the road to judgment.

"It was a real pleasure seeing you again, Bob," I said. "Good luck on judgment day and in eternity. I do hope you'll get to play catch with your dad again."

We shook hands, and a friendly smile once again returned to his face.

"It was great seeing you again, Tony," he said. "I think I remember that hit you got off me in the mid 1980s."

"I bet you do," I said with a chuckle.

I watched him as he made his way back on to the road to judgment. Before he merged into the throngs of marchers, he turned around and waved, and I caught one last glimpse of his red cap and Chief Wahoo on the bill of it.

"Goodbye, Heater from Van Meter," I said to myself.

CHAPTER 19

Wilt Chamberlain

When I returned to the road to judgment, I noticed myself surrounded by thousands of World War I and II, Korea, Vietnam, Union, Confederacy, Gulf War, and Afghanistan-era soldiers. As we marched along, I noticed how some wore muddy boots and bloodstained uniforms, their faces caked with dirt and grime. But yet many wore freshly starched U.S. Army or U.S. Marines fatigues with spit-shined boots. Their dog tags jingled from their necks. Some wore helmets, and some didn't.

I wondered why the disparity. Was it because some died instantly in battle and didn't have the chance for a nice funeral? In my mind, they were all heroes. I recognized unit insignias on their shoulders. There were soldiers from the 1st and 9th Infantry Divisions, 1st Air Cavalry, the 1st Marine Division, and the 82nd and 101st Airborne Divisions. I hoped I would see the famous Audie Murphy again, the most decorated soldier in World War II, as we walked.

I really felt out of uniform in my hospital garb, but no one seemed to care. Some of these men had been dead hundred of years and longer. They all either nodded or smiled as they passed by me. I nodded and smiled back. We were all headed to the same place, and nobody seemed eager to engage in a big conversation. We seemed to have walked some distance when I noticed a huge man shooting hoops on a basketball court located just off the road. He reminded me of a giant walking tree, and I immediately recognized the man I had met in San Diego in 1973.

It was the NBA's Philadelphia 76ers legend Wilt Chamberlain. He had passed away in 1999 at the age of sixty-three.

I had met "Wilt the Stilt" when I worked for former Ironman Al Couppee at KGTV-TV in San Diego. Wilt had come to the station for an interview, and I remembered how he had to "bow" his head when he walked into the sports department. He was the biggest human being I had ever seen in my life. Not only was he tall at seven feet and one inch, his arms and thighs were massive and resembled tree trunks. Nonetheless, he wore a big smile on his face when Al introduced me to him.

We shook hands, and my hand was dwarfed by his. His hand was easily twice the size of mine. He was at least a foot taller than me and I had to stare up at him. I remembered his head had almost grazed the office ceiling.

I debated whether to interrupt his shooting and then I thought I should at least say hello. I saluted the veterans, wished them all well, and left the road to judgment. I proceeded down some steps to the most picturesque basketball court I had ever seen. It had beautiful glass backboards with a freshly buffed hardwood floor. The grass around the court was beautifully manicured, and there was a field nearby filled with different colored tulips. It reminded me of Tulip Time in Pella, Iowa, in early May. A rose garden was also located nearby. It was a scene tailor-made for eternity.

Wilt was dressed in a Harlem Globetrotters uniform. He had played for them for a short stint before his magnificent pro career. He wore a blue shirt with large red letters on the front that read "Harlem Globetrotters." He was dressed in white-and-red-striped shorts and red-and-white-striped socks. Brilliant white tennis shoes covered his huge feet, and I wondered how big they were. He whirled the basketball in his giant hands at the free throw lane and then, with one colossus step, leaped and dunked the ball through the white threads of the basket. It made a loud *swoosh* sound.

"Hi, Wilt," I called out. "I'm Tony Powers. I worked for Al Couppee in San Diego in the 1970s. I met you at Al's station when he was the sports director there. You came to the station to promote your new volleyball league. I was thrilled to have met an NBA icon."

He stopped shooting, held the basketball in his hands, stared at me for a long moment, and sized me up. He looked more like he was thirty-three than sixty-three with massive shoulder and arm muscles.

"You worked for Al?" he asked.

"Yes, back in 1972 and '73," I said.

"He was a great guy," he said. "I enjoyed watching his sports-casts. I remember he'd interviewed me a few times. What did you do there?"

"I was a sports producer. I shot and edited film of games and went out with the cameramen to do interviews outside the station," I answered.

"Is Al still alive?" he asked.

"No, he passed away some years back," I said. "In fact, I bumped into him up here and we had a nice visit. He looked great, and I got to thank him for hiring me and helping me start my sports broad-casting career."

He had a puzzled look.

"You saw Al up here?" he asked. "How was that possible?"

"I don't know, Wilt. It surprised me too. I've met all kinds of icons up here, including you. For some reason, the Good Lord has let me recognize them and talk to them. We all have the same thing in common, whether we're celebrities or not. We're all on the road to judgment."

"Amen to that, brother," he said. "It seemed like I've been on that road forever, but as you can see I took a little break to shoot a few baskets." He chuckled. "What happened to you, Tony, and when did you pass away?"

"I passed on in 2014, this year, Wilt. I mean, I think it's still 2014. I had minor knee surgery and something went terribly wrong. I guessed it was just my time to go," I said.

A surprised look showed on his face.

"You mean I've been gone over fifteen years?" he said.

"Gone but never forgotten, Wilt the Stilt," I said. "Your hun-dred-point game in 1962 will never be broken. Even guys like

Michael Jordan, Kareem Abdul Jabbar, Kobe Bryant, and LeBron James could never break it. I mean, you averaged fifty points and twenty-five rebounds a game for the old Philadelphia Warriors and 76ers. Those were incredible numbers, Wilt, even though Jabbar eventually broke your NBA career scoring record of over thirty-one thousand points. You're still the man.

"I remember the NBA had to change their free throw rules to include no dunking because you could dunk a free throw. You stood behind the free throw lane and then leaped into the air all the way to the basket and dunked it. They didn't know what to think," I said with a laugh.

A big smile emerged across his face. He had extremely white teeth. He still had movie star looks, even in eternity. Then the smile gave way to a more somber look.

"Thank you for the compliments, Tony," the big man said. "My numbers won't mean a thing to God. I still have to go one-on-one with him, and I'm sure I'll lose bigtime. I made a lot of mistakes in my life that I regretted. I hope that he'll have mercy on me. I had a big reputation on earth but it means nothing up here. I'm sure you heard all the stories and rumors about how I dated over thousands of women in my lifetime."

"He's very merciful," I said. "I never believed those stories. It was probably a few sportswriters hoping to write a sensational story and they got carried away. First of all, I think it would have been physically impossible to have cavorted with that many women," I said with a grin.

"I hope for my sake the Good Lord didn't believe those stories," he said.

"He won't because he's all-knowing," I said.

I wanted Wilt the Stilt to shoot more and I had an idea.

"How about a game of H-O-R-S-E, Wilt, and no dunking allowed?" I suggested.

His laugh seemed to echo throughout eternity, and he fired the ball toward me.

"You're on. Bomb away," he said with a chuckle.

I caught his pass, took a couple of dribbles to the three-point line, and launched a twenty-footer toward the basket.

Saaaaawish was the sound it made as the ball sailed through the nets.

An amazed look filled Wilt's face as he readied for his shot.

"I didn't know I'd be facing a ringer," he said with a laugh.

He fired from long range and the ball clanked off the rim, skirted off the court, and into the tulips.

"H," I said triumphantly.

I missed my next five shots in a row, and Wilt made all of his to win easily. He even included a couple of Michael Jordanesque moves around the basket. He also got me with a couple of free throws he shot underhanded, something he was very good at in the NBA. We both worked up a sweat, and I marveled at how this huge physique of a human being could be so agile. He seemed to glide before suddenly spring about four feet into the air. *Wow*, I thought to myself. I had just gone one-on-one with an NBA icon.

He thought he'd better return to the road to judgment after our game. I agreed I should too.

We shook hands, and my mind drifted back to San Diego when I had first shook hands with this giant. His hand dwarfed mine again, but he was very careful not to squeeze my hand too hard.

"It was a real pleasure to have met you again, Tony," he said. "I hope God is very fair with you in eternity."

"The pleasure was all mine, Wilt," I replied as I stared up at him. "Good luck to you too."

He handed me the ball and with about three big strides made his way back up the steps and back on to the road to judgment. As he drifted away, the Harlem Globetrotters theme song echoed in my ears.

"Goodbye, Wilt the Stilt," I said as he disappeared into a throng of humanity.

I turned and faced the basket once more before I returned to the road to judgment. I fired off another jumper toward the rim from around eighteen feet away.

Saaaaawish.

CHAPTER 20

Amelia Earhart

After I had merged back into the line on the road to judgment, I again wondered who I would meet next in eternity. As I walked along, I looked around for a familiar face. I noticed a middle-aged woman wearing a brown leather flight jacket with white pants and shiny black boots that stretched almost to her knees. She had big eye goggles that rested on the top of her head. She was smiling and having an animated conversation with an older gentlemen dressed in flight overalls, brown boots, and similar eye goggles that sat on the top of his head.

It couldn't be, I thought. *It just can't be.*

As she drew nearer, I recognized the woman I had read about for years and whose picture I'd seen in numerous books, newspapers, and magazines. She was the first woman ever to fly solo across the Atlantic Ocean, the great Amelia Earhart.

She had disappeared in July, 1937, at age thirty-nine in her attempt to become the first person to fly around the world. The last time they were heard from, she and her navigator, Fred Noonan, were attempting to fly to Howland Island in the Pacific Ocean. There have been numerous theories about what had happened to them. Did they run out of fuel and were forced to land on some Pacific atoll? Was their plane intercepted by the Japanese and they were taken prisoner? Did they become lost, run out of fuel, and drown when their plane crashed into the Pacific? Did they survive when the plane went down and they lived for a while on some small Pacific Island?

The reporter in me wanted to find out.

They were only a few feet from me when I called out.

"Aren't you Amelia Earhart?" I asked.

They stopped short and stared at me.

"I am, sir. With whom do we have the pleasure?" she said.

"I'm Tony Powers from West Des Moines, Iowa."

"Glad to meet you, Iowa," she said with an animated face. "I'm Amelia, and this is Fred Noonan."

We all shook hands. I couldn't believe I was in the presence of this strikingly beautiful woman and her handsome friend. She didn't look older than twenty-five. She had short red hair, gray eyes, and nice white teeth. Fred was in his midforties, had reddish-brown hair, stood about six feet one inch tall, and had piercing blue eyes.

I couldn't think of anything to say right off; I merely stared at both of them.

"I know. You're wondering what happened to us out in the Pacific Ocean," she said as both of them grinned widely, breaking the silence.

"It was on my mind," I said. "But my mother always told me never to pry even though I was a sports reporter down there on earth. Everyone on earth wondered what happened to you two. There were numerous books written about you. One report said the Japanese captured you after your plane ran out of fuel and ditched in the Pacific Ocean. You both became prisoners of war. Then someone circulated a photo which showed the back of a woman who sat on a dock surrounded by Japanese soldiers. They reported the woman could have been you."

They both looked at each other and laughed heartily.

"Fred, did you know we were prisoners of war once?" she said, laughing.

"No, dear," he said. "If the Japanese did save us after we ditched, then what are we doing up here?" He laughed.

"Another report stated you ran out of fuel," I said. "You then swam to a small, deserted island nearby and lived out your days until your bodies were eaten by giant crabs. They reported only some bones were found."

They again howled with laughter.

"This is getting very interesting, Fred," she said. "Please continue, Tony."

"Those are just a couple of the theories of what happened to you," I said. "But that was many years ago. You both could have died from old age by then."

They both had surprised looks on their faces.

"What year did you pass away, Tony?" he asked.

"This year 2014."

"What!" Amelia gasped. "Wait a minute. We attempted to fly around the world in 1937. You mean we've been gone seventy seven years?"

"Yes. If you both had lived, you would be well over one hundred years old by now," I said. "So it doesn't really matter now what happened to you two back then, does it?"

"No, it doesn't, Tony," she said with a somber tone. "We just can't believe we were lost at sea nearly eighty years ago. It seemed like yesterday that we began this road to judgment."

"Amelia, you and Fred were certainly considered pioneers in your day," I said. "God will recognize you for that. He'll reward you both for helping to advance mankind. Your spirit and determination helped set the stage for women adventurers for years to come. Did you know we have women pilots flying commercial passenger jets now? We have women astronauts orbiting the globe somewhere up here in a space station. We can't forget you, Fred. You inspired men to become pilots and astronauts. Did you know we have landed men on the moon since both of you disappeared? We're on the verge of sending men and women astronauts to Mars. You two may have passed on but you both left legacies that will be remembered for years to come."

"If only I had a second chance at life," Amelia said with a forlorn look. "I wouldn't have wasted a second of time. I would have spent more time with my family and prepared myself better for judgment day. Gosh, I can't believe we've been on this road for seventy-seven years. We could be on it for another seventy years," she said, looking at the long lines ahead of them.

"Ditto," Fred added.

"One year, one hundred years, five hundred years, even centuries can go by very quickly up here," I said. "There is really no time but God's time up here. He is omnipresent. He will judge each of us on what we accomplished on earth. He will certainly give you two credit for helping make mankind and the world a better place."

"What do you think God looks like, Tony?" Amelia asked.

"Well, I had a picture of him on my fireplace mantel at home. When you looked at the photo straight on, God resembled an older man with a beard and long hair. Then when you looked at the picture another way, his image changed to a young man with short hair. I imagine he could be a cross between the two. Remember, he's all-knowing, all-powerful, all-merciful, and all-forgiving. I read in the Bible that we have absolutely no idea what God has planned for us. It will be so great that we can't imagine it. I can't wait to meet him."

"How did you die?" she asked. "You must have passed on in the emergency room or in the hospital."

"Would you believe too much anesthesia may have done me in," I said with a laugh. "I went in for minor knee surgery, and that was it. Did both of you guys drown?" I asked, hoping to finally find out the secret of their disappearance seventy-seven years ago.

They both looked at each other and smiled, then looked back at me.

"You said it doesn't really matter now how we died, does it, Tony?" Amelia said.

"You know, you're right," I said. "The past is past, and meeting the Almighty is most important right now."

"We should continue our march to judgment, Tony. Thank you for your encouraging talk and and for letting us know where we stand in eternity. We will never forget you," Amelia said, leaning over to give me a nice hug. "God bless you."

"Tony, thank you for your wisdom," Fred said, also giving me a hug.

"Thank you, guys," I said. "It was fantastic meeting you. I've read so much about you. I'll pray for you both."

I watched as they turned around and merged back into the long lines that headed toward judgment day. They seemed to melt away into the large throngs of people. What if I got back to earth and said I had met Amelia Earhart and Fred Noonan in eternity? I thought. I would be in all the newspapers and on all the radio and television talk shows.

But the secret of how Amelia Earhart and Fred Noonan disappeared in the Pacific Ocean would remain with them throughout eternity.

CHAPTER 21

Dic "Youngsey" Youngs

It seemed I had no sooner returned to the road to judgment when I heard goldie oldies music emanating from inside a crowd of people walking behind me. I slowed my stride a little to let them catch up. They were a mixture of gray-, white-, and dark-haired folks dancing their way to judgment day. I had to laugh. They looked like they were having the times of their lives. The men either had slicked-back hair or crewcuts and wore white slacks and flowered shirts with white socks and white shoes. The women wore mostly blue sweaters with knee-length pink skirts and white socks and loafers. Most of them had ponytails. It looked like a scene straight out of the hit movie *Grease*.

When they had caught up to me, I stepped aside to watch them dance. The music was deafening. "Sheeeeeeeerry, Sheeeeeeeerry baaaaaaby." The song blared away, then I heard a very familiar voice that boomed from a microphone. I couldn't believe it. Somewhere in the throng of the swirling dancers was "Youngsey," the legendary disc jockey Dic Youngs. He had passed away in 2009 at age sixty-eight.

"That's the hit record 'Sherry' by Frankie Valli and the Four Seasons," he announced. "Put on your dancing shoes, folks, we're going to rock into eternity. Here's Three Dog Night and their hit song, 'One.'"

He emerged from the crowd of dancers and held a wireless microphone. It was Dic in his prime. He wore a white short-sleeved shirt with a scarlet tie, dark slacks, and white socks with brown Hush Puppies. His black hair was neatly trimmed, and he wore his trademark mustache. He was slimmed down and didn't appear a day over forty. When he noticed me, his expression changed like he had just seen a ghost. He was so surprised. Then he tilted his head back and chuckled.

"Tooooneeee Poooowers," he said over the music and dancing. "I'm shocked, old buddy. I'd never thought I'd meet the WHO natural athlete here in eternity. When did you arrive here, my old friend, and where did you get those clothes?" he asked as he shook my hand vigorously.

"Hello, Youngsey," I said in a loud voice. "I had knee surgery that went bad in 2014 and I passed so quick that this is all I had on when I came up." I laughed.

"You do have something on under that hospital shirt, I hope?" he said grinning.

"Yes, I'm glad I do," I laughed. "I'd give anything for a pair of pants and white socks and shoes."

"Just a second. I've got to introduce another song," he said.

He brought the microphone up to his lips and in his classic announcer's voice ordered another oldie.

"That was 'One,' by Three Dog Night. Here's the talented Leslie Gore and her hit single, 'It's My Party and I'll Cry If I Want To.' I met her numerous times, folks, and she's one heck of a lady. Here's 'It's My Party.'"

I elevated my voice again to speak over the music.

"Dic, I'm sorry I didn't have a chance to visit you before you passed. You had a big funeral with many of the former KIOA Good Guys in attendance. You're a broadcasting legend and icon. I remembered when I grew up on a farm and I used to listen to you on my transistor radio while I did the chores. You're one of the main reasons I chose to become a sportscaster. I wanted to be on the radio just like you and do play-by-play," I said. "I've met all kinds of sports icons and famous people up here, Dic, and you're right at the top of the list, my dear friend."

He stared at me a long moment, and I noticed his eyes get a little watery and cloudy. I thought for a moment he was going to cry.

"Thank you, my friend," he said. "I struggled with my health for a long time before I finally passed on. But I had a fantastic life and have no regrets. I wanted to become a disc jockey ever since I was eleven years old and became one when I was only sixteen. I loved to make people laugh and be happy, and that's why I hope God will give me credit for that on my judgment day. As you can see, we've had a great time up here already and I hope we can do this for all eternity. I miss my wife and family and all the Good Guys and Women I worked with. I'm so glad that I made a difference in your life, Tony."

"You certainly did, Dic," I said. "You were my inspiration when I listened to you growing up on the farm. You're in the Iowa Rock 'n' Roll Hall of Fame, and I hope someday you'll be recognized and inducted into the National Rock 'n' Roll Hall of Fame with the big golden oldie stars. You helped raise millions of dollars for charity, and I'm sure the Good Lord will look favorably on that."

The Leslie Gore song had almost ended, and he spoke into the microphone again to introduce another oldie.

"That was Leslie Gore, ladies and gentlemen. Now let's wind it down a little bit and do a little slow dancing, and remember, don't get that close to your partner because we're in eternity, folks, and God and his angels are watching us," he said with a grin and a wink. "Here's Bobby Vinton with one of his big hits, 'There! I've Said It Again.'"

I chuckled at his line and wondered where the music was coming from. I didn't notice any giant jukeboxes or speakers around.

"Dic, where's all the music coming from?" I asked.

"You'll have to ask God about that, Tony," he said with an amused look. "Remember, we're in eternity and anything's possible up here."

"You were quite an athlete in your prime, Dic, and in high school for the Des Moines East High Scarlets. You were an all-city quarterback in football and an outstanding baseball player as well. You even became a disc jockey while still in high school. You captained the KIOA High Hoopers basketball team for years. I remembered when our WHO Owls played your team before a Dallas Cowboys basketball exhibition game at Valley High School in the 1980s. You guys won, but I surprised you with a behind-the-back pass for a basket," I said.

"That's why I always called you a natural athlete," he said with a smile. "I really enjoyed watching you, Pete Taylor, and Heidi Soliday do the sportscasts."

"Thank you so much, my friend, for the tribute but I'm not looking for any accolades up here, Dic," I said. "I left all that behind on earth. Up here, God's going to know how I lived my life. He'll judge me on how well I lived it. I made plenty of mistakes, Dic, and I hope he forgives me."

He placed both of his hands on my shoulders and looked me dead in the eyes.

"What do you think it will be like, Tony?" he asked.

"You mean when we finally meet God?" I said.

We turned and looked at the millions of souls walking toward the magnificent cloud in the distance.

"I don't exactly know, Youngsey, but it will be wonderful, I think. That's all I can tell you."

"Tell me again how you died?" he asked. "How could a big, strapping, healthy guy like you suddenly pass away?"

"That's just it, Dic," I said. "I don't know if I'm really dead or not."

"You mean God is giving you a short preview tour first," he laughed.

"All I know is I had a chance to play some golf with Coach Johnny Orr up here on a golf course that looked like Augusta National. Johnny went into the clubhouse and came out dressed in fabulous golf knickers. He couldn't get any for me to wear because they told him I hadn't qualified yet. In other words, Dic, I took that to mean that I wasn't quite dead yet," I said.

Dic had a look that resembled someone just struck by lightning.

"You mean you're somehow gravitating between eternity and earth," he said with a portentous look. "And you played golf with Johnny Orr! Unbelievable!"

"And I threw some passes with Nile Kinnick, shot arrows with Olympic gold medalist Doreen Wilber, traded baskets with Wilt Chamberlain, received some jelly beans from President Ronald Reagan, and met the legendary Amelia Earhart, to name a few," I said.

Dic had another look like he was about to faint. But how could he faint when he's already dead? I thought.

"Tony, it sounds like you're having the time of your life up here," he said. "Do you really want to go back to earth?"

"It depends on what God wants, Dic, not me," I said.

"He'll forgive you, Tony, and he'll forgive me and all these great folks dancing around us. All we have to do is ask for forgiveness. I don't know about you, but I could do this for the rest of eternity. Look at all the fun these people are having as they dance their way down the road to judgment. You sure you don't want to join us as we continue our trip?" he asked.

"I'd look kind of funny dancing around in my hospital shirt, Dic," I said, laughing.

He smiled and pulled me close to him and gave me a big bear hug for a moment.

"So long, my friend," he whispered into my ear.

"So long, Dic," I replied.

He turned around and put his microphone again to his lips.

"Okay, folks, let's get moving on the road to judgment again. Let's speed it up with my old buddies the Beach Boys and their hit song, 'She's Real Fine My 409.'"

The music blared out, and the dancers leaped into the air at the sound of the new song as they continued their way down the road to judgment. Dic was right in the middle of them and it looked like he had the most fun of all. It reminded me of the movie *The Wizard Of Oz*, where Judy Garland and her friends danced their way down the Yellow Brick Road. I watched until they had disappeared into the distance and the music had faded out.

I thought of Dic's classic line that he used at the end of every one of his broadcasts.

"Thank you everybody for turning me on."

CHAPTER 22

Jesus Christ

I decided I had better start walking a little faster if I was ever to reach judgment day. As I walked, a gentleman wearing a hooded brown robe and sandals came up alongside me. He looked to be in his early thirties, had a short beard and mustache, and had dark, penetrating blue eyes. He reminded me of one of the disciples in the Old Testament spreading the word of God to the crowds in the desert. He seemed to know me.

"Hi, Tony," he said.

"Do I know you?" I asked.

"I hope so," he replied.

"How did you know my name?" I asked.

"I've known everything about you, Tony, from the moment you were born up to now," he said.

I suddenly felt the most nervous that I ever felt in my entire life. I shook with anxiety as I took another long look at the person walking beside me. He walked on my left side, and I noticed the hole in his right wrist and the hole in the middle of his right foot. *Oh my god*, I thought.

My mind was frozen with fear. What do you say to your Creator? What do you say to the person who was crucified and died on the cross for you? What do you say to the Almighty who knew every moment of your life and all the sins and transgressions you committed? What do you say to the person who knew you before you were even born? What do you say to this person who knew every second of your life?

He seemed to know that I was all tied up in knots and speechless.

"Don't be afraid, Tony," he said. "I'm not going to harm you."

"I don't know want to say, Lord," I replied.

"You don't have to say anything," he said. "Just walk with me."

We walked and walked, and I was surprised that none of the millions walking with us recognized this man. They all streamed by, intent on getting to the big cloud in the distance. I finally worked up the courage to speak to him.

"Lord, how could you be with me when so many people are walking by us to meet you in judgment day?"

He laughed a Godlike laugh.

"Tony, didn't you know I'm omnipresent? I can be here walking with you and also judging people in the cloud ahead."

"In other words, you can be in two places at once?" I asked.

"Something like that," he said.

"Lord, am I really dead and are you going to judge me here in eternity?" I asked nervously.

"That's what I wanted to visit with you about, Tony. In answer to your first question, no, you're not dead. You've still got some time left on earth. I wanted to give you a little preview of what to expect in eternity. I want you to go back to earth and proclaim my name and do my will. Of course, people will not believe you if you tell them you've seen me in eternity. I want people on earth to believe what they have not seen, not what they have seen. You're one of the few who have seen, Tony, and believed."

"But what about all the famous people on earth I've met in eternity, Lord? Former presidents, athletes, coaches, and actors like Presidents George Washington, John Kennedy, and Ronald Reagan? And Nile Kinnick, Harry Caray, Bob Feller, and the others. Were they real? Did I really talk with them?" I asked.

"Oh yes. I wanted you to meet them in eternity. I wanted them to tell you how they missed their lives on earth and if they could go back to earth how they could rectify any wrongs they committed. I'm giving you the chance to go back, Tony, and tell people to clean up their lives and believe the good news. Encourage people to keep obeying the Ten Commandments and do good works and believe in God, Tony."

"Thank you, Lord," I said. "I'm ready to go back and spread the good news. But what can I do? I'm only one man. You're right, Lord, no one would believe me if I went back to earth and told folks that I had met you in eternity and we had talked. They'd think I was a crazy man."

Jesus stopped and turned toward me, and I could see some sadness and despair in his eyes.

"You don't have to do that, Tony," he said. "Just go back and lead by example. Be the best person you can be. Always help and assist others. Obey my commandments and support St. Peter's church on earth by attending and supporting your own church. I know you are a member of the Knights of Columbus. Stay faithful to that. Be Christlike in everything you do, Tony. Goodbye, my friend, I'll see you later in eternity."

After he said that, he simply vanished into thin air.

I never felt so happy in my entire life.

CHAPTER 23

It Wasn't a Dream!

Just as I was propelled into the heavens when I was first anesthesized, I suddenly felt myself being propelled back toward earth. I had a tremendously peaceful feeling. Had I really just seen God and walked and talked with him? Why had he chosen me to give a preview of eternity? Just like St. Thomas the apostle, I had seen the holes in his hands and feet and believed. I remembered the gospel saying, "Blessed are those who have not seen and have believed."

Mother Earth looked beautiful as I got closer and closer. I looked back over my shoulder and could see the millions in the distance going to their judgment day. I was glad to have been given more time on earth. A brightness like an airliner's landing light soon enveloped me. I strained my eyes to see through it. What was it? I thought. What the heck! I suddenly realized I was staring into an overhead operating room lamp.

A female voice reverberated in my ears.

"Tony, wake up. Are you awake, Tony? You've had a nice sleep for the last couple of hours. How do you feel?" the voice asked.

I blinked my eyes a few times and a young nurse with black hair pulled up into a bun on her head stared down at me. She looked to be in her midtwenties and wore a green head cover and green scrubs. She had a nice smile and very white teeth. Wait a minute, I thought. I was just on the road to judgment with all these other humans of all ages, sizes, and colors, and some with their animal friends. I was one of millions of souls that walked in a human traffic jam on a continuous road that stretched far into the heavens and disappeared into a giant, illuminated white cloud. How did I end up back on a hospital bed?

"Are you feeling any pain in your knee?" she asked.

Oh my god, I thought. *I'm not dead. I'm aliiiiiiive.* What happened to eternity? You mean it was all a dream? I couldn't have been dreaming, I thought again. I met all those wonderful people and sports icons. I talked with them about their lives and their families and how they had lived their lives on earth. They were real people who laughed and cried. It couldn't have been a dream. It was so real. I played golf, threw passes, shot arrows, and played basketball. I hugged them and shook their hands.

I got to know them so well in just a short amount of time. Or did I spend an eternity and not know it? I wanted to cry but at the same time I was elated that I woke up and found myself back on earth. Everybody that I had met in eternity wished that they could have had more time on our wonderful planet Earth. If only they had been given a second chance at life, they told me. How precious their lives were. Had I really been dead for a while? Did I actually make the trip to eternity before I was called back for some reason? Or was it all in my imagination, an anesthesia-induced dream?

"Are you feeling all right?" she asked again.

"Yes, but my mouth feels very dry. I don't seem to feel any pain in my knee," I said. "But were there any complications in my surgery? Perhaps my heart might have stopped and I needed to be resuscitated?"

She gave me an odd and puzzled look, then smiled.

"Oh, heavens no," she said. "Why would you ask that? You were out cold and slept like a baby. Once the anesthesia hit your lungs, you were gone."

"That's what I meant," I said. "Was I really gone?"

"You mean you dreamed you were dead?" she asked with an astonished look on her face. Then she chuckled.

"I dreamed I was in eternity," I said. "I met all these great and famous people. Nile Kinnick, JFK, Ronald Reagan and his dog Lucky,

George Washington and his soldiers, even Christopher Columbus. And I saw Joan Rivers and Bob Hope."

"Wow," she exclaimed with a smirk. "You've got some imagination, Tony. I wish I could dream like that. You should tell the surgeon about your experience when he comes to visit you. He'd probably find it very interesting. Other patients have told me they couldn't remember anything. Yours must have been a wonderful dream, though. The anesthetics they use to put you to sleep these days are very powerful.

"They basically come in two types. Those that cause unconsciousness and those that deaden a part of the body while you're still semiconscious. You were knocked out completely because they had to work inside your knee. Now let's get you out of bed and into a wheelchair, shall we?"

"It was a wonderful and beautiful experience I had meeting all those folks," I said with a sigh.

"I bet," she said as she helped me into a wheelchair. "Maybe you should write a book about it," she said with a laugh.

She probably thought I was half nuts.

I sat in the recovery room and reflected about the famous icons I had met in eternity and how each one had affected me. Were my conversations with them real or just figments of my imagination? Had I been in some sort of limbo where I was half in this world and half out of it? Had the powerful anesthesia affected my brain and memory cells? Did God really call me, then change his mind? Had he really given me a preview of eternity?

Meeting JFK, John Fitzgerald Kennedy, our thirty-fifth President of the United States, was a wonderful surprise. No doubt he would have been one of our greatest presidents had he lived longer. I've often thought he had one of the greatest quotes of any U.S. president in history. "Ask not what your country can do for you; ask what you can do for your country." Brilliant.

It was my opinion that the Russians had brainwashed Lee Harvey Oswald to assassinate him. JFK had made the Soviet Union back down when he stopped them from building ballistic missile sites in Cuba, just ninety miles from the U.S. coast. President Kennedy had made the Russians blink first in a showdown, and they resented that, in my opinion.

When I had spotted the great Heisman Trophy winner and Iowa Star Nile Kinnick on the road to judgment, it was the thrill of a lifetime. I'd often dreamed as a sportscaster of being able to interview him and see him live as a football player. We had a great conversation in eternity, and to have been able to play catch with him was a dream come true. I'll never forget how excited he was when I told him Kinnick Stadium in Iowa City had been named after him. It was a shame they never found his body or plane. He died a real hero. Next time you're in Adel, Iowa, drive down Nile Kinnick Drive.

I was pleasantly surprised when I bumped into the legendary Iowa State and Michigan basketball coach Johnny Orr in eternity. We had had some great interviews when he was alive, and I loved it when he called everybody "coach." Having been able to play a round of golf with him in eternity on a course that resembled Augusta National was unbelievable. And to see the great Bob Hope, Payne Stewart, Jack Benny, and Ben Hogan on the golf course as they played ahead of us was a thrill beyond words. Had he not been one of the greatest college basketball coaches ever, Johnny could have played on the Champions Tour as a professional golfer.

To have seen Jim Duncan, the greatest voice ever of the Drake Relays, on the road to judgment certainly made my visit to eternity a memorable one. I was so privileged to have known and interviewed him numerous times in Drake Stadium after the Relays. He was ecstatic when I told him that they had named the track in the stadium after him. I'd always remembered when he told me once that we're all replaceable and expendable in life. He was right.

To have met the iconic actor and war hero Audie Murphy was a "wow" moment for me. I so wish I had known him in real life because we were both combat veterans who suffered from posttraumatic stress disorder, or PTSD. I bet I have seen every one of his Western movies. What he did to win the Medal of Honor in World War II was absolutely incredible, killing and capturing almost an entire company of German soldiers. He was awarded every medal our country and military had. I know God will offer him one more award. He'll get to spend eternity with the Almighty in heaven. So long, Audie, I hope you consider me your friend always.

I was so happy to have seen the 1976 Olympic gold medalist Doreen Wilber on the road to judgment. Who would have imagined that this woman from small town Jefferson, Iowa, would have become one of the top female archers in the world? She was also a world-class pie maker. I licked my lips as I remembered the time I had interviewed her in the backyard of her home in Jefferson. She had baked one of her classic apple pies for me and my photographer. It melted in your mouth; it was so good. I even brought some of it back to WHO-TV for Jim Zabel. If they awarded a gold medal for making pies, she would have won a couple more.

I was thrilled beyond belief when I saw our fortieth President of the United States, Ronald Reagan, in eternity. All I had to say was "WHO" and he and his giant dog Lucky walked right up to me. He had loved WHO and gushed with enthusiasm as he recalled his days as a sports announcer for the station. What more could another person have accomplished in life? I wondered. WHO Radio Sportscaster, Hollywood actor, governor of California, and the fortieth President of the United States. I was so fortunate to have worked at the same radio station that he had. And he loved jelly beans. I do too.

When I saw the legendary Bill Reichardt as he headed to judgment day, I was embarrassed to have been dressed in only hospital clothes. He was always impeccably dressed in one of his Reichardt's or Mr. B's suits. He kidded me about my hospital garb and laughed about it. In life, he was never afraid to speak his mind and offer his opinion. I thought how incredible it was that he was named the 1951 most valuable football player in the Big Ten Conference despite having played on a team with a losing record. How many times has that ever happened? He was a wonderful clothier, football and handball player, politician, inventor, and, most of all, a great human being. I was fortunate to have known him.

I had always wanted to meet the Drake football icon Johnny Bright. I did in eternity. He was one of the greatest players in Drake and Canadian Football League history. I surmised that if he had played in the NFL, he'd probably be in the league's Hall of Fame today. His broken jaw incident will be remembered forever in the annals of college football as a despicable act. But in eternity, he told me that he had forgiven his attacker. He was very happy that Drake had named its football field after him. I really wished I had met and known him in real life. What an incredible person.

I thought about how it had been a great privilege to have bumped into UCLA's basketball coaching icon John Wooden in eternity. I reminded him of the time when I had walked around the corner of Pauley Pavilion while covering the West Regional in Los Angeles and almost bumped into him. He probably didn't remember it, but it was no doubt one of the highlights of my sports broadcasting career. He was very gracious as I reintroduced myself to him again on the road to judgment. His memory was unbelievable as we talked about former Iowa Basketball coach Tom Davis and Iowa State's Johnny Orr. He even remembered playing Drake in the Final Four. What a thrill to have visited with the greatest college basketball coach in the history of the game.

When I met the famous aviator Amelia Earhart and her navigator, Fred Noonan, in eternity, I thought I would finally solve one of the mysteries of the world on how and why they disappeared over the Pacific Ocean in 1937 in their attempted flight around the globe. We found out after our visit that it really didn't matter. They were very amused when I told them what the press thought about their death. But what was really important to them on the road to judgment was meeting God. I was so fortunate to have met these wonderful folks in eternity. Whatever happened to them will remain a mystery forever.

I had always wanted to interview the legendary actor and pro football star Alex Karras when I was a sportscaster. That's why I was especially thrilled to have met the former Iowa star in eternity on the road to judgment. I was impressed at what a humble human being he was. He wasn't a bit upset at not having been selected to the NFL Hall of Fame despite having been the league's most dominant defensive tackle for years with the Detroit Lions. He didn't care because he was about to meet God. I learned that when you're in eternity, it didn't matter whether you were inducted into the Hall of Fame or not. It's how you lived your life that counted. I'll never forget him.

I still can't believe I met the father of our country and our first president, General George Washington, in eternity. I saw that he was a fearless leader and his men would follow him forever even in eternity. They had marched on the road to judgment a long time, and I hoped the Good Lord would be fair to each and every one of them. I was never more thrilled that when I had saluted the general, he and his men returned my salute. You'll never meet a prouder American than me after that.

When I saw the man who first hired me in broadcasting, Iowa Ironmen legend Al Couppee, in eternity, I was almost overcome with emotion. He was one of the men to whom I owed my entire sports-casting career. He took a chance when he hired me, and I think he did it because I was from Iowa like he was. When I told him I had met Nile Kinnick in eternity, he broke down momentarily into tears. No other human being had had such an effect on Al in this world as Nile. Coup, as they called him, was a big man who reminded you of Santa Claus without the white beard. I knew the Good Lord would be very fair to him on judgment day. I hoped God would unite him with Nile Kinnick again so the two could spend eternity together. Thank you, Al, for everything you did for me.

When I crossed paths with North Carolina State basket-ball coach and legend Jim Valvano in eternity, it was a very special moment for me. I was very blessed to have interviewed him in life before he was struck down by cancer. His famous speech at the ESPYS will be remembered forever as a call to arms against the disease. We laughed when I kidded him that he looked like a guardian angel on the road to judgment. Seriously, maybe that's what the Good Lord will appoint him as someday. His famous words, "Don't give up, don't ever give up," will resonate through the ages and be a reminder to anyone who's had to overcome maladies or diseases in their lives. Fight on, coach!

I had always wanted to meet the man who had discovered America, Christopher Columbus. I had read about him in sixth grade history class at St. Joseph's elementary school in Des Moines. I got my wish in eternity. He was a fantastic-looking swashbuckler who was as eager to meet me as I was to meet him. There's a difference of opinion on who actually discovered America. Some say the Norsemen did it, but I told him I thought he was the one who had the credit. He laughed and said that was good enough for him. This man was a later version of the twelve apostles. He helped spread the Word of God and Christianity to a pagan New World. He was thrilled when I told him we celebrated Columbus Day every October in his honor.

I was so happy to have crossed paths with Jim and Tait Cummins on the road to judgment. Jim was a wonderful reporter and bureau chief for NBC News. His uncle Tait was a broadcasting legend for WMT Radio in Cedar Rapids and a sports writer for the *Cedar Rapids Gazette*. I had known Jim very well in life and I would have loved to have known Tait when he was a broadcaster. I had heard plenty of stories about him from his nephew Jim. Especially those that involved Tait's play-by-play. He not only described the action on the field but what happened in the stands, on the sidelines, and in the parking lot. They were two broadcasting icons to remember.

Any baseball aficionado knows the name of Bob Feller, and I was so fortunate to have met him on the road to judgment. He had an incredible adventure in life, which started when he played catch with his dad on the farm growing up. Who knew he would become one of the most recognizable stars in major league baseball history for the Cleveland Indians. He ranks right up there with the likes of Babe Ruth, Casey Stengel, Mickey Mantle, Lou Gehrig, and Joe DiMaggio. I chuckled to myself when I thought about the base hit I got off him in a media game in the 1980s. He wouldn't admit that he made the pitch so easy to hit that a twelve-year-old Little Leaguer could have done it. Thank you, Heater from Van Meter!

When I played H-O-R-S-E with NBA and Harlem Globetrotters legend Wilt Chamberlain, I marveled at the grace and fluidity of this giant of a man. He either just flipped the ball into the basket or he'd knock down a twenty-foot jump shot with ease. He was as wide as he was tall on his over-seven-foot frame. His tennis shoes resembled snowshoes because his feet were so large. Wouldn't it be funny if God had to stare up at him on judgment day? I thought. But I doubted that could ever happen. He was a humble person despite his greatness on earth. I felt it was a shame that some sportswriters and columnists had labeled him a ladies' man on earth. He had the look and smile of a movie star. He was. I thought he was great in *Conan the Barbarian*.

My trip to eternity wouldn't have been complete without seeing my old friend and world-class disc jockey Dic Youngs. This rock 'n' roll icon personally knew all the old-time rockers of the '50s and '60s and brought most of them to the world-famous Iowa State Fair to perform in his oldies shows. While growing up on the farm, I listened to his golden oldies show while doing the chores. I wanted to be a disc jockey too, but sports announcing won out. He had a great voice and personality and passed away way too early. *He'll keep them rocking in eternity*, I thought with a smile.

Who can forget the late, great Harry Caray? What a thrill to have met one of baseball's all-time great announcers in eternity and reminisce about his days as the legendary Chicago Cubs announcer. It was a shame that he never broadcasted the Cubs in a World Series. When I covered a Chicago Cubs-Los Angeles Dodgers series in the mid-1980s at Wrigley Field, I met Harry for an interview. He was a great interview. He thanked the Iowa Cubs, Chicago's top farm team in Des Moines, for sending up so many good players to Chicago. Half of Chicago's roster were former I-Cubs. I sat in a booth next to his broadcast booth and watched more of him than the actual games. He'd yell, "Holy cow!" into the microphone after a great Cubs play. He was a class act that we'll never forget.

CHAPTER 24

Eternity or Figment of My Imagination?

As I sat in the recovery room waiting to be released by the doctor, I stared at my left knee, which had been wrapped tight with a large bandage. I decided I wouldn't even mention my visit to eternity to the doctor. I thought about how when I first entered the surgery room I was struck by the shape of the operating table. It looked like a big, solid, steel crucifix, a T shape in the middle of the room with a giant spotlight shining down upon it.

I had climbed onto the table, and the nurse helped spread out my arms and legs. I thought about how Christ had died on a wooden cross. I was laid out on a steel cross. It was so cold that I shivered and goose bumps formed on my arms and legs. The nurse smiled and told me to relax. They had to keep it chilly in there so germs couldn't spread, she said. She placed a hard rubber mask over my face and told me to breathe deep. I was instantly propelled into outer space and the heavens. Our planet Earth appeared so beautiful and the oceans so blue. I felt like an astronaut without a space suit. Was it all a dream or had God purposely granted me a preview or vision of what was to become?

Had my life flashed before my eyes, as the old saying goes? Could I have passed on and returned to earth before anybody knew I was gone? Had the anesthesia transported me into another state of consciousness? Or had my nervousness before the surgery let my imagination go overboard? The wonderful people I had met in eternity seemed so real and human. All the millions of people and their animals who marched on the great road to judgment knew they were all headed to the same place. They all knew they were going to be judged by God on their judgment day.

As I stared at my bandaged knee, I reconciled that it must have been one giant dream. I was alive and breathing and the folks I had met in eternity had been gone for years. As I pondered this, the pretty nurse with the bun hairdo suddenly appeared and told me the surgeon would be in to see me shortly. She also had something in her hand and asked me if it belonged to me. She had discovered it in the pocket of my hospital shirt after surgery.

They were three jelly beans—one was red, one was white, and one was blue.

ACKNOWLEDGMENTS

I want to thank the famous people, coaches, and sports icons who inspired me to write this book while they were alive. The photos of some of these famous people were very instrumental in the book, and I want to thank the University of Iowa and Iowa State University for the bust photos of Nile Kinnick and Johnny Orr. I want to thank WHO Radio for the photo of President Ronald Reagan.

When my novel went to press in 2020, these were some of the events that happened after 2014.

Former First Lady Nancy Reagan passed away in 2016 and joined her husband, President Ronald Reagan, in eternity.

Alex Karras was finally inducted into the 2020 National Football League Hall of Fame.

The Chicago Cubs won the World Series in 2016, defeating the Cleveland Indians four games to three. "Holy cow!" Harry Caray would say.

There is an ongoing movement to change Columbus Day on our calendars to Indigenous Peoples' Day.

Production has started on a Hollywood movie about the life of Nile Kinnick.

The Drake Relays, 2020 Summer Olympics, and many other sports were cancelled or delayed in 2020 due to the COVID-19 pandemic. A terrible virus that killed thousands of people around the world.

If Audie Murphy were alive today, he'd be ninety-six years old.

This is a work of fiction. I do not claim I underwent a real near-death experience, only what might have happened had I experienced one.

Tony A. Powers

© USA TODAY Sports

© USA TODAY Sports

© USA TODAY Sports

© USA TODAY Sports

© USA TODAY Sports

© USA TODAY Sports

© WHO Radio

© WHO Radio

ABOUT THE AUTHOR

Tony A. Powers is a former radio and television sportscaster at WHO Radio and TV in Des Moines, Iowa. He worked at the same radio station as the late president Ronald Reagan. Some highlights of Tony's broadcast career included covering the 1984 Summer Olympics in Los Angeles and the 1986 Rose Bowl. He also made an appearance on the former NBC hit show, *Bloopers and Practical Jokes*. Tony is a decorated Purple Heart U.S. Army veteran and survived a traumatic brain injury in combat. Tony is the author of two mystery novels, *Murder on the Opinion Page* and *1st and Dead*. He and his wife, Connie, reside in West Des Moines, Iowa.

Lightning Source UK Ltd.
Milton Keynes UK
UKHW011920260122
397754UK00001B/216